THE BRAZILIAN GROOVE BOOK

KIKO FREITAS

SAMBA & BOSSA NOVA

Edited by Joe Bergamini
Design and layout by Rick Gratton
Cover design by Mike Hoff
Transcriptions by Kiko Freitas
Music engraving by Lucas Brum
Executive Producer: Rob Wallis

For the musical examples inside the book:
Acoustic guitar and bass: Kiko Freitas
Pandeiro and snare drum brush loops: Kiko Freitas

All the video and audio recordings (drum tracks): Audio Porto Studios
Recording engineer: Rafa Hauck Video mixing and editing: Jean, Lauro, Shi, Rodrigo, Douglas and Pedro (Audio Porto Crew)

Photography by Júlio Cordeiro (p. 27, 28, 31, 32, 34, 35, 39, 42, 50, 51, 57, 61, 65, 76, 77, 95) and Lauro Alves PY3EB (p. 23). All other photos from author's personal collection.
Cover Photos by Júlio Cordeiro

HUDSON MUSIC

Copyright © 2020 Hudson Music LLC

SONG CREDITS
Tanajura (João Bosco & Francisco Bosco)
João Bosco - Acoustic Guitar & vocals
Armando Marçal - Percussion
Robertinho Silva - Percussion
Ricardo Silveira - Guitar

Rio (Nelson Faria)
Nelson Faria - Acoustic Guitar
Cliff Korman - PianoCafé - Percussion
David Finck - Acoustic Bass

Brasilified (Cliff Korman)
Written by Cliff Korman
Copyright ©2001 Almonds and Roses Music (BMI)
All rights reserved. Used by permission

Cliff Korman & Nelson Faria's book *Inside the Brazilian Rhythm Section* is available from Sher Music Co. www.shermusic.com

Nelson Faria - Acoustic Guitar
Cliff Korman - PianoCafé - Percussion
David Finck - Acoustic Bass
Brooklyn High (Nelson Faria)
Nelson Faria - Guitar
Ney Conceição – Bass
www.cliffkorman.com

Brooklyn High (Nelson Faria)
Nelson Faria - Guitar
Ney Conceição – Bass

To Download Audio for this Book:
Go To: halleonard.com/mylibrary
Enter Code: **1129-8211-8548-6055**

Contents

Dedication

I would like to dedicate this book to these wonderful people who have been a shining light in my life.

To the memory of Aldir Blanc, the great master of the words.

To the memory of the great Wilson das Neves, a true master in the art of Brazilian drumming.

To the memory of my first drum teacher, Argus Montenegro.

To my mother, this project is also dedicated to my mother, Beatriz de Castro, who showed me the way and allowed me to go in search of my dream.

To Colin Bailey, a master in the art of jazz drumming, whom I have the honor to call my friend.

Special Thanks

To Rob Wallis and Hudson Music for the partnership and invitation to release this book.

To João Bosco and Aldir Blanc for their sublime and unique contribution to the music world.

Special thanks to all the great Audio Porto crew who also made this project possible.

Very special thanks to Lucas Brum, whose work putting my text and drum parts into the computer was an essential part of this book.

Many thanks to Paiste Cymbals, Vic Firth Drumsticks, Pearl Drums, Gavazzi Cases and Urban Boards for their support and care.

To Daniella Brunelli for her kind presence and help with the text.

To my dear Marco Nazari for our three decades of friendship.

To my friend and partner in many projects, Pedro Lima.

To all the drummers in Brasil who, despite having many difficulties, keep searching for the development of Brazilian music.

To my father, Telmo De Lima Freitas.

My deepest thanks to the Great Source of all things, creatures, life, light, music and inner rhythm of the universe. "The truth is only One, the Masters call it from many names."

About this Book

The idea of this book is to give an up-close view and comprehension of my application of the Brazilian rhythms on the drum set. I have developed these grooves during the 33 years of my career as a professional drummer, with 20 of those years playing with Brazilian legendary composer, singer, and guitar player João Bosco.

This book contains exercises to develop the independence in order to play the Brazilian styles with more confidence and comfort, allowing you to explore your own creativity.

It is my opinion that listening is the most important thing in music. Like any other language, we start listening to other people talking and then, little by little, we start developing our vocabulary to finally speak the language naturally, with fluence. It is very important to listen to the great masters of Brazilian music in order to "dive" deeply into the vast ocean of this music.

For me, music is a living energy and a deep form of communication. I am so grateful for being a musician, for all the great people I got to know through music, the many wonderful places I saw and all the light and energy music brings to my life. I feel so blessed to have been playing with and listening to so many wonderful musicians throughout my life, with whom I learned and still learn so much. I thank them all very deeply.

It is impossible to talk about Brazilian music without talking a lot about rhythm and about Africa. And, coming form a percussive root, all Afro/Brazilian styles have this aspect of conversation and "trust-each-other" feel between all the players—just like a tribe.

Since the 15th century, unfortunately, more than 15 million people were brought as slaves from Africa to the "New World" of America. More than 80 percent went to Brasil and the Caribbean Islands. Fifteen percent went to the Spanish colonies in Central and South America. Only 5 percent went to the United States. We can barely imagine the many different peoples, cultures, religions and languages (like Umbundo, Quimbundo, Quicongo, Ioruba, etc.) mixed up in the colonies. I believe rhythm and music comprised the little common ground for all the people coming from the distant Africa.

From this initial sadness, however, a very rich reality was born: Brasil is a big mix of music, colors, sounds, religions, rhythms, ethnicities, culture and language accents. Like the great poet Vinícius de Moraes said, "Samba is the sadness that swings."

The Rhythmic Collective Unconscious

I really believe there is a common ground unifying the rhythms of many cultures, countries and continents. Invisible and unnamable rhythmic archetypes live inside the hearts of many different human beings and nations and are the responsible for the foundation of the many rhythms and music styles of the world.

Some old tribal beats resonate in our souls when we listen to Brazilian rhythms, a tribal beat from Angola, a drum solo by Elvin Jones, a tabla player playing in a Kirtan or the old Taiko drums from Japan. Some of these rhythms may perhaps receive a different name from their original source, and this name can vary from place to place (or even inside the same country; Brasil has continental dimensions, for example). But there is some mysterious pulse communicating through the rhythms, trying to tell us a story, trying to awaken inside our souls the old fires from ancient times.

Some of the rhythmic cells in this book can tell you a story, activate the old fire inside your heart and can, I hope, make you feel the joy of music and rhythm while you study and practice them. Have fun!

Kiko Freitas

Ways to Practice

It is very important to sing all the rhythms and combinations before you play them. For example, sing the basic tamborim pattern while you play the written combinations on the bass drum or snare drum. By doing this, you develop your inner independence and time, and also can have a deeper connection with the rhythms you are practicing.

Always remember that listening is the best way to internalize and learn any style of music. Many times, what is written doesn't correspond exactly to the sound you are hearing. The written grooves are a reference guide to what you hear, that's why is so important to listen to a lot of recordings and live performances in the style you are studying.

Music can't be found on a piece of paper. It can only be found inside yourself.

Drum Key

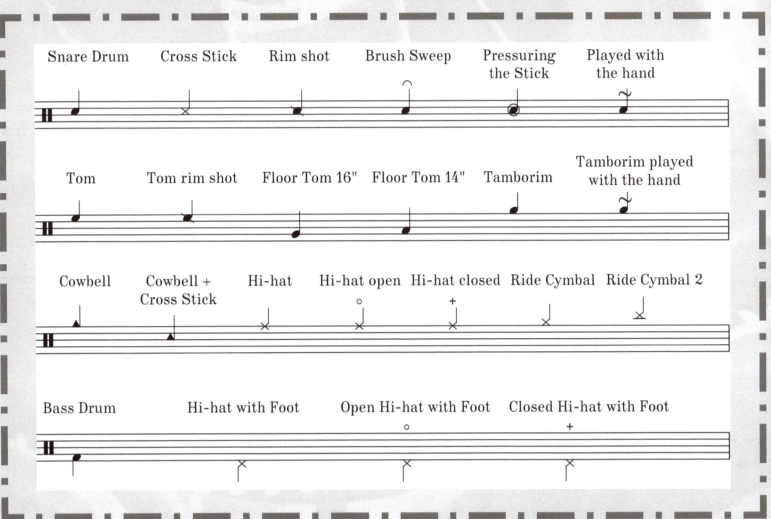

Part 1: Samba Layers

I like to think about the Afro-Brazilian rhythms as "layers" of sounds that speak to each other, creating a rhythmic conversation. Music is a language, and it is very important to listen with attention before you start talking, just like we do when we start to learn a new language.

We basically have 3 layers of sounds in samba: the low layer, the middle layer and the high layer.

A) Low Layer: This layer of sounds is the responsible for the pulse of samba, giving the basic foundation of the time and groove. The low layer is formed by three surdos (instrument very similar to a floor tom): first surdo, second surdo and third surdo.

The *first surdo* is the lowest pitched instrument in samba. This instrument is responsible for playing the second beat of the 2/4 measure, the strongest part of the samba rhythm.

The *second surdo* is a little higher pitched than the first surdo and plays the first beat of the 2/4 measure of the samba rhythm.

Here we have the first surdo:
Fig. 1

And here we have the second surdo:
Fig. 2

In the example below, we have the first and second surdos playing together:
Fig. 3

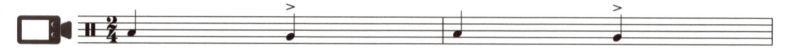

The third surdo is the smallest of the three surdos and it is also the highest pitched. This surdo plays figures between the two quarter notes played by the first surdo and second surdo. Each samba school has a different pattern to this instrument. The *third surdo* "cuts" between the first and second surdos, therefore it is also called the *cutting surdo*.

Here is a basic example of the third surdo:
Fig. 4

In my drum set application of the three surdos playing together, I play the first and second surdos with my right hand and the third surdo with the bass drum.
Here is the example:
Fig. 5

B) Middle Layer: This layer of sounds is formed by the instruments that keep the sixteenth-note feel flowing in the samba groove. Snare drums, repiques, pandeiros and ganzás (shakers) are the main instruments in this layer. For the drum set application, the knowledge of different snare drum patterns and the Brazilian sixteenth-note feel is very important in order to understand the groove completely.

Here is a basic example of a snare drum samba pattern. It is very important to listen to recordings of this style in order to internalize the real feel, because the notation does not communicate the "soul" of what is played:

Fig. 6

Here is a snare drum pattern I have created to mix the snare drum with the repique feel, leaving the right hand free to move between the snare drum and the toms, also using rim shots and different "colors" of the instrument:

Fig. 7

Here we have a groove using the snare drum, the toms and the bass drum, creating a mix of the low layer and middle layer of sounds:

Fig. 8

C) High Layer: This layer of sounds is responsible for the syncopations of samba. The melodies of the good sambas are based on this layer of sounds and its instruments, specially the tamborim. Agogôs, cuícas, frigideiras and repiques are also important instruments in this high layer of sounds.

When I mix the high layer with the bass drum and the snare drum, I use the *marcha clave*, normally played with the left foot, as you can see here:

Fig. 9

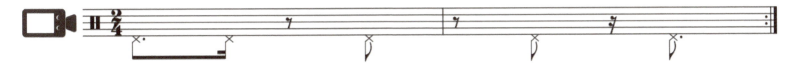

Here we mix all three layers in one groove, remembering it is very important to sing the individual parts of the groove while you play another part. For example, you can sing the marcha clave while you play the snare drum pattern; sing the tamborim pattern while playing the bass drum, etc...

Fig. 10

In the heart of Portela Drum Line.

Part 2: Independence Applied to Samba – Using Tamborim Drives

I must discuss a very important "voice" in the samba world: the *tamborim*.

The tamborim is a small percussive instrument, but with a huge importance in Brazilian music. All the good samba melodies are based mainly in the tamborim patterns.

The tamborim is the inseparable companion of the great samba composers, the acoustic guitar players, the small batucada ensemble and also is considered the violin of the samba orchestra—a "Escola de Samba." When I play the tamborim patterns on the drum set, I will use the hi-hat, cowbell or ride cymbal. But when the tamborim is played by a single player, there is a special technique to be explained.

The middle finger of the hand which is holding the instrument plays ghost notes, and also exerts occasional pressure on the head while the other hand is playing, which mutes the sound of the stick or finger (when the tamborim is played using the index finger, in a very soft situation).

Here is a written example of this way of playing the tamborim:

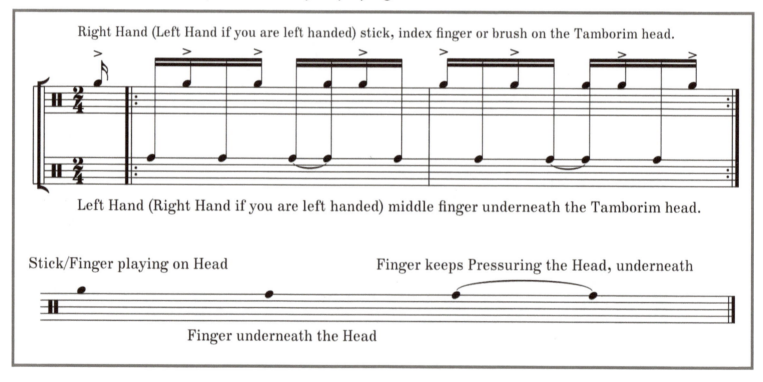

Of course, when you play the tamborim figures in a drum set situation, you can't play the finger underneath the head, so you'll play only the main syncopations with the sticks or the brushes.

Here are some exercises to develop and improve your independence playing samba. I encourage you to create new grooves by mixing the different percussive cells shown, always trying to apply the grooves in a tune, in order to check if you are achieving the right feel.

It is very important to understand and feel the basic tamborim pattern. I recommend singing all the basic samba patterns while you play the tamborim figure and then singing the tamborim pattern while you play the other written subdivisions, like the bass drum and the snare drum patterns. This will help you to feel the rhythm, internalizing all the details and subdivisions of the style. I always remember the great masters telling us, "If you can't sing, you can't play."

Here is the basic tamborim pattern played on the hi-hat:
Fig. 11

As you can see, this is a two-bar feel, starting syncopated in a pickup measure, playing the fourth sixteenth note before the first beat of the first bar. I use to say that the great majority of the good sambas ever composed use this kind of "airy" syncopation and pickup measure. Almost all the great samba composers used to play the tamborim or the tamborim pattern on a match box to create their tunes. I like to compare this pattern with a small conversation, a kind of "question and 21 answer" thing. The first bar stars with the fourth sixteenth note on the offbeat and the second bar starts with two eighth notes on the downbeat.

Now we will sing the first, second, third and fourth sixteenth notes separately while we play the tamborim pattern. It is important to practice each exercise many times, at a slow tempo, before moving to the next exercise, always singing each one of the parts.
Fig. 12

Part 2: Independence Applied to Samba-Using Tamborim Drives

Here is an example in which I play the tamborim pattern on the hi-hat and sing the whole idea of the groove, thinking about the snare drum and bass drum sounds:
Fig. 13

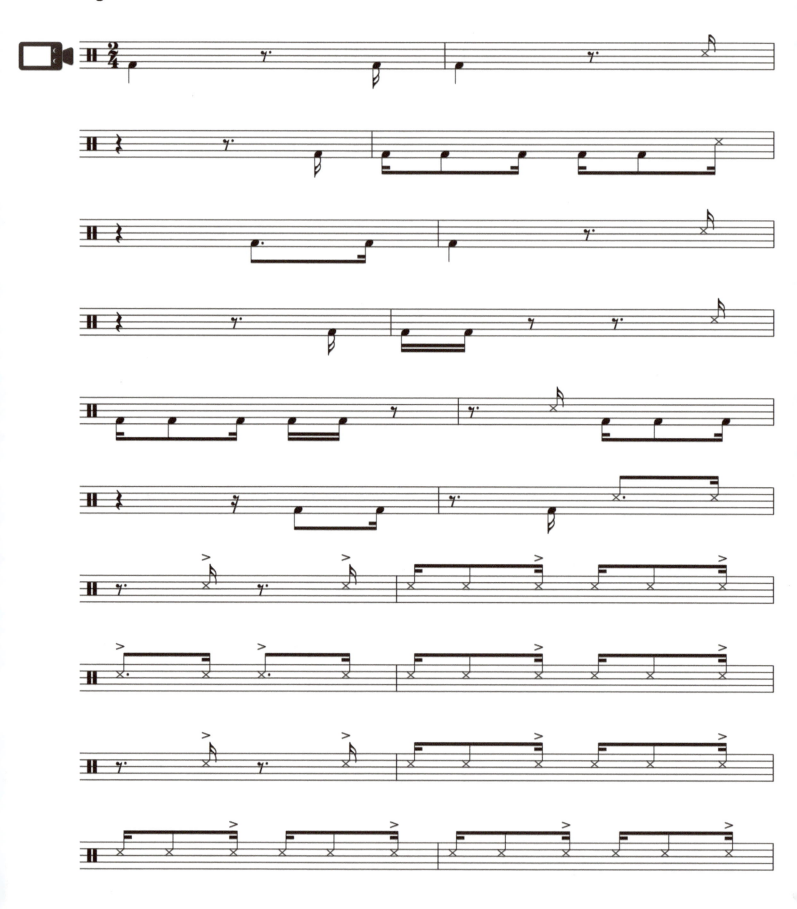

Recording the surdo in Hamburg, Germany, for the *Olympic-Games of Passion* CD with the NDR Bigband. Music composed and arranged by Wolf Kerschek.

Part 2: Independence Applied to Samba-Using Tamborim Drives

After singing the four sixteenth notes individually, we play them on the snare drum, bass drum and hi-hat, while we continue to play the tamborim pattern with the right hand. It is also very good to sing the tamborim pattern (before playing it) while you play each one of the sixteenth notes on the bass drum and snare drum:

Fig. 14

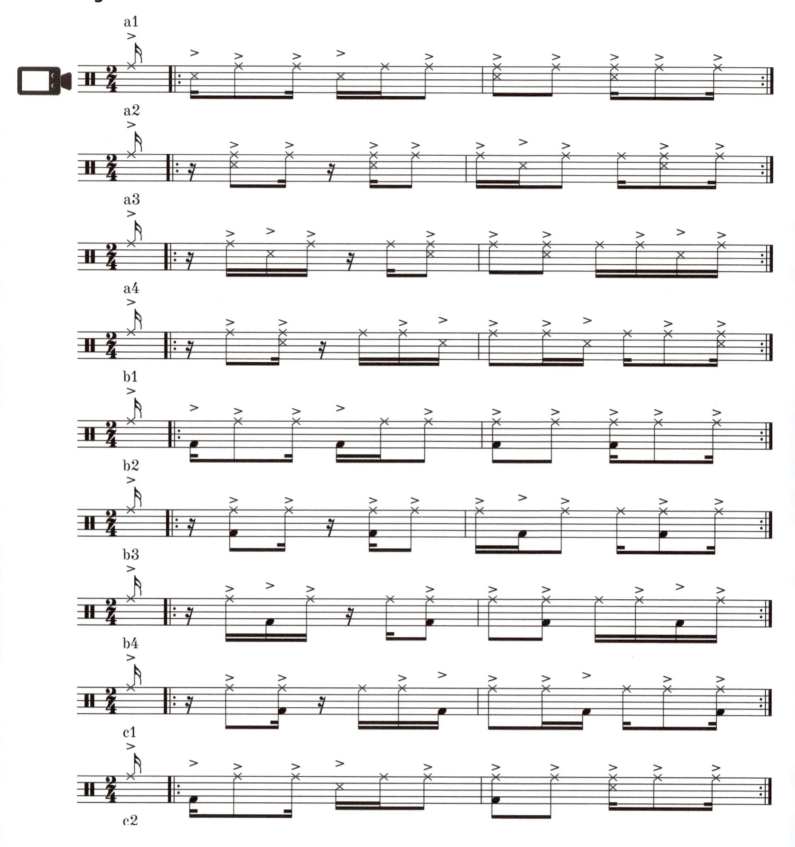

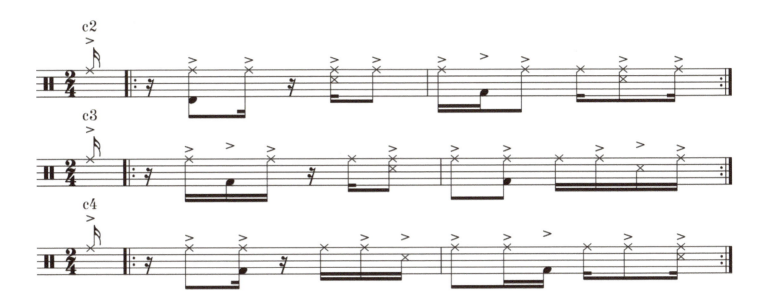

After you feel comfortable playing the tamborim pattern and singing each one of the four sixteenth notes separately, we can move on singing groups of two sixteenth notes (1st and 2nd, 2nd and 3rd, 3rd and 4th & 4th and 1st), while always keeping the tamborim pattern going.

Fig. 15

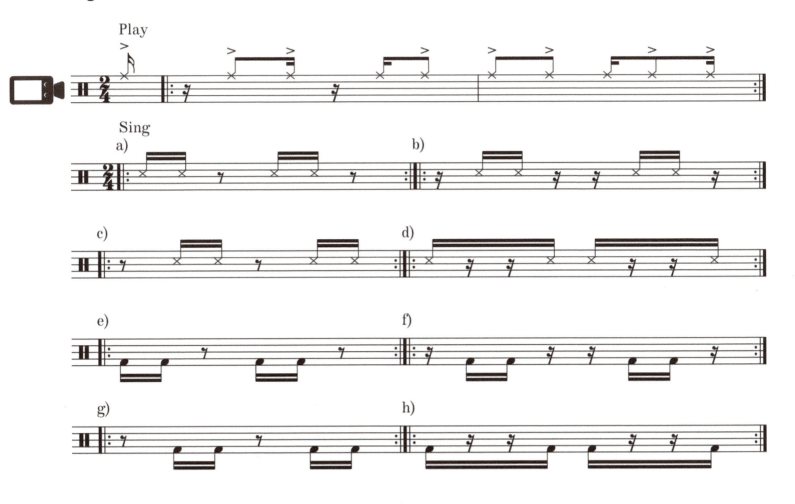

Part 2: Independence Applied to Samba-Using Tamborim Drives

Putting the tamborim pattern (played on the hi-hat) and the groups of two sixteenth notes played on the snare drum together, we have the example below (always remember to practice very slowly and with a metronome):

Fig. 16

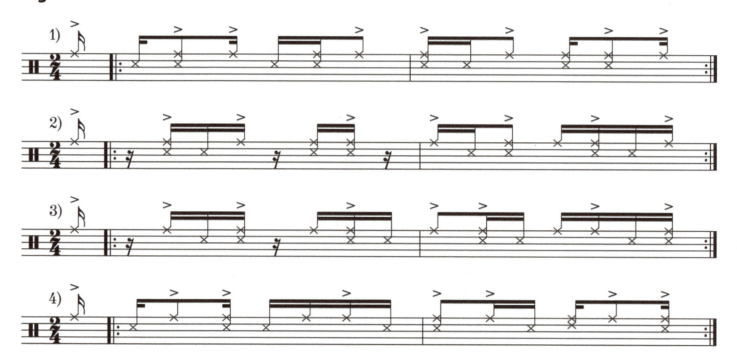

Then we can move the snare drum notes to the bass drum:

Fig. 17

After you sing and play all the four sixteenth notes individually and in groups of two sixteenth notes (while playing the tamborim pattern), you can start to sing combinations of the sixteenth notes with a samba flavor, like this:

Fig. 18

It is important to sing the same example while playing the tamborim part many times, until you feel comfortable with the pattern, before moving to the next example.

After you feel comfortable singing all the combinations while you play the tamborim pattern, start playing the combinations using the snare drum and the toms, while you keep playing the tamborim with the other hand. You can play the tamborim figure with the closed hi-hat or ride cymbal, combining it with the snare drum and toms.

Below are four options to use the bass drum along with the tamborim and snare drum combinations, practicing one at a time, slowly and trying to feel the samba atmosphere going on.

When I play the first and second surdos using the bass drum, I use an up-and-down movement with the foot. For the second surdo, which plays the first beat, I play an upstroke using the heel up motion and pressing the beater against the bass drum head, creating a softer sound. For the first surdo, which plays the second beat (the stronger beat in samba), I play a downstroke, using the heel-down motion and releasing the beater from the head, creating a full-bodied sound, like this:

Fig. 19

Fig. 20 – Bass Drum Technique + Tamborim

On the following page there is an interesting little batucada with a 32-bar form. The tamborim pattern is played on the cowbell with occasional notes moved to the toms. The hi-hat opens and closes with the foot (splash sound).

Fig. 21 – Small Batucada Groove

Part 2: Independence Applied to Samba-Using Tamborim Drives

After you feel comfortable playing the tamborim pattern while you sing the four sixteenth notes individually, all the written combinations (Fig. 18) and the bass drum patterns (Fig. 19), it is time to combine all this percussive voices in a samba groove. In the next example, I will combine the tamborim (played on the hi-hat) with one of the snare drum combinations plus one of the bass drum patterns.

Fig. 22 – Tamborim + Snare Drum **a**

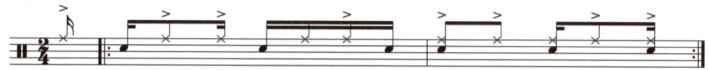

Fig. 23 – Tamborim + Snare Drum **b**

Fig. 24 – Tamborim + Snare Drum **a** + Bass Drum **b**

Fig. 25 – Tamborim + Snare Drum **b** + Bass Drum **a**

Fig. 26 – Tamborim + Snare Drum **h** + Bass Drum **d**

Fig. 27 – Tamborim + Snare Drum **c** + Bass Drum **c**

After you practice the different voices creating grooves with the closed hi-hat, you can practice all the combinations playing the tamborim pattern on the ride cymbal using these different hi-hat options with the foot, mixing them with the snare drum combinations and bass drum examples:

Fig. 28

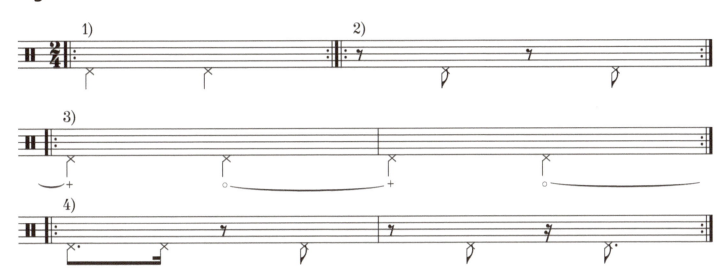

Here, as an example of the four independent voices, mixing the tamborim played on the ride cymbal + combination i) + bass drum d) + hi-hat 4 (always remembering it is very important to sing each individual part along with the tamborim pattern before you play the complete groove and before you read the drum part as a visual block):

Fig. 29 – Tamborim + Snare Drum **i** + Bass Drum **d** + Hi-Hat 4

Now let's add a snare drum pattern with more movement along with the tamborim pattern, played on the tamborim. I use this combination often with the great samba master João Bosco:

Fig. 30

Adding a different bass drum and hi-hat pattern, we have another version of the groove. The groove can be heard on the tune "Incompatibilidade de Gênios" on the *Obrigado Gente* DVD by João Bosco (2006, Universal Music).

Part 2: Independence Applied to Samba-Using Tamborim Drives

Fig. 31 a

Fig. 31 b

Fig. 31 c

Adding some more movement to the snare drum, we can have interesting figures and colors, while keeping the tamborim pattern on the cowbell with the right hand and the two surdos with the bass drum:

Fig. 32

Rhythm is meditation.

Photo by Lauro Alves PY3EB

Part 3: Left Foot Independence

Here are some examples of how to develop independence for the left foot on the hi-hat. A good idea is to play (and first sing) the tamborim pattern (here played on the cowbell) while you play each one of the sixteenth notes with the left foot independently.

Photos: Júlio Cordeiro

The following examples are to be played with the left foot (right foot if you are lefthanded) using the hi-hat or a cowbell played with a pedal. The idea is to have more freedom to develop your creativity and fluidity when you play the grooves.

Fig. 33

Fig. 34

This next example goes "over the barline" with the 2/4 samba groove:

Part 3: Left Foot Independence

When you feel comfortable playing the tamborim pattern together with each one of the sixteenth notes played on the hi-hat with the left foot, you can try playing a full samba groove with the cowbell, snare drum and bass drum while playing the hi-hat foot on each individual sixteenth note, like this:

Fig. 35

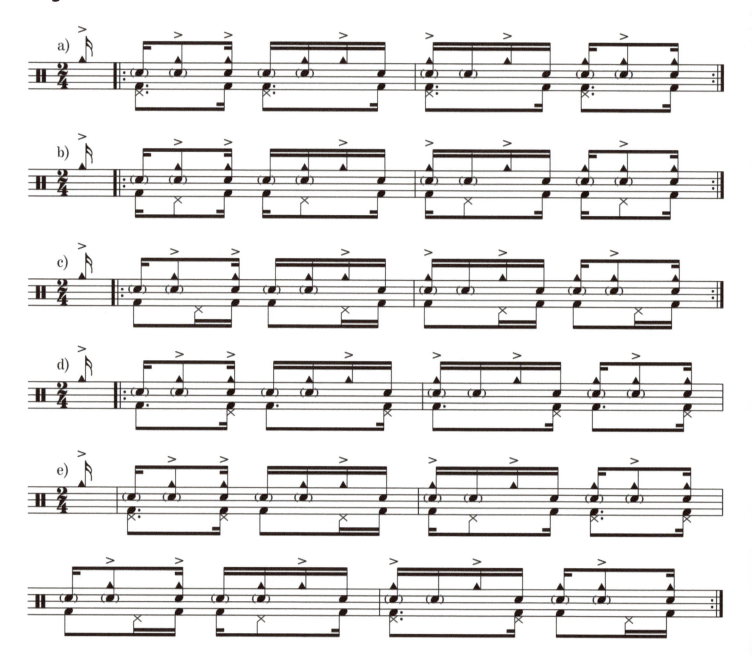

If you continue playing this groove, the hi-hat will be playing "over the barline" in a 4/3 pulse.

Here is an example of independence for the hi-hat in 7/8. The hi-hat creates a different pulse that goes over the barline, completing the idea after three bars while the right hand keeps playing the tamborim pattern in 7/8 on the ride cymbal. It's very important to sing the 4:3 pulse while you play this example:

Fig. 36

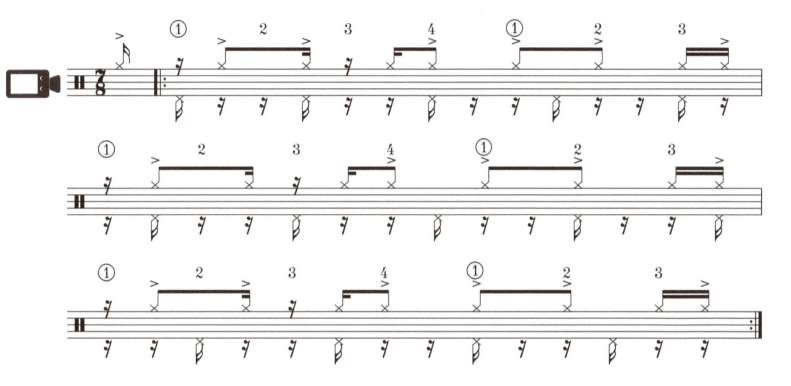

Photo: Júlio Cordeiro

Part 4: Independence - Left Hand Patterns + Combinations

Photo: Júlio Cordeiro

Now we are going to practice the tamborim pattern with the left hand while playing different combinations against it with the right hand (if you are left-handed, practice the tamborim with your right hand and the combinations with your left hand). It is important to sing the combinations while playing the tamborim pattern before you play the patterns with your right hand.

Now we are going to practice the tamborim pattern with the left hand while playing different combinations against it with the right hand (if you are left-handed, practice the tamborim with your right hand and the combinations with your left hand). It is important to sing the combinations while playing the tamborim pattern before you play the patterns with your right hand.

The bass drum and hi-hat will play this pattern throughout all the combinations:
Fig. 37

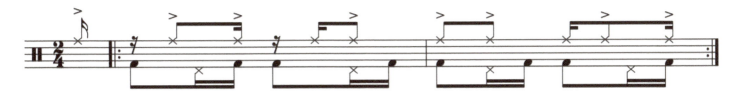

Here we have the combinations to practice with the tamborim pattern, bass drum and hi-hat.

Practice each exercise many times, slowly, before you move to the next example. Remember to sing the quarter-note pulse while you practice each one of the examples.
Fig. 38

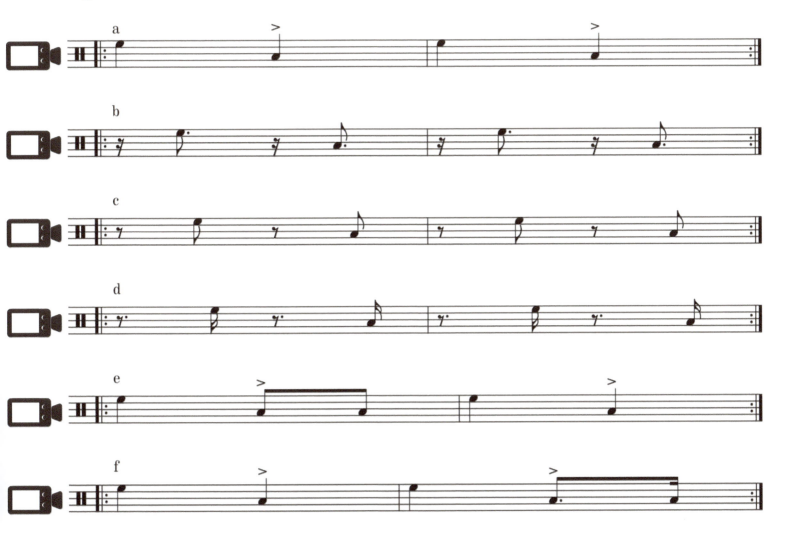

Part 4: Independence - Left Hand Patterns + Combinations

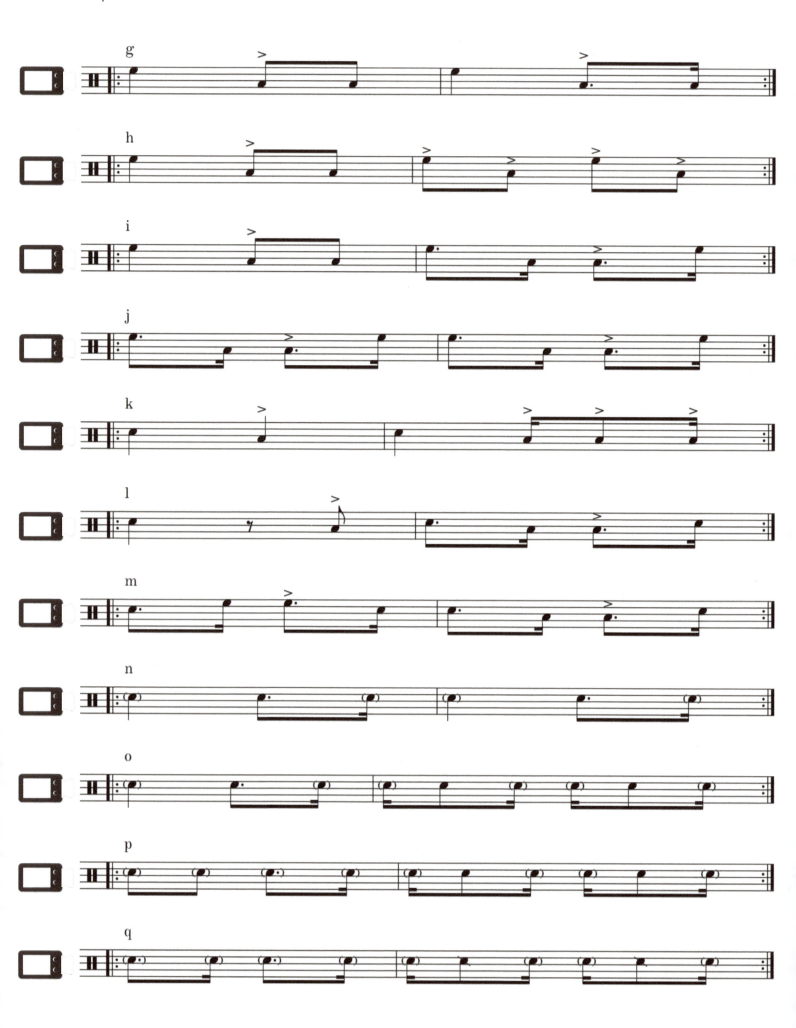

Now, in a 32-bar form, we can mix the different combinations in one musical idea, improvising a little with the right hand while keeping the tamborim pattern with the left and bass drum/hi-hat ostinato:

Fig. 39

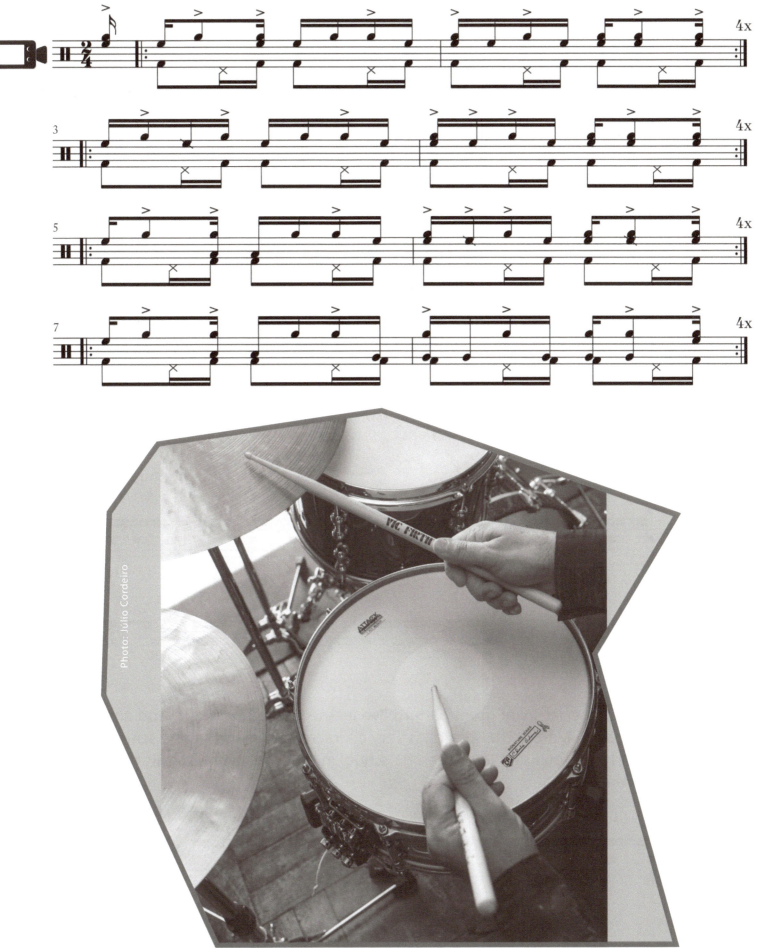

Photo: Júlio Cordeiro

Part 5: Samba Snare Drum

The snare drum is a very important instrument in Brazilian music. It was brought to Brasil by the military forces who came to defend the territory, in the dawn of Brasil. Some snare drum patterns, mixed with native Brazilian and African rhythms, created the foundation of many Brazilian rhythms. It's very important to internalize the feel of the various snare drum patterns to understand the samba feel. Below are some examples that I use frequently when playing this style of music; the bass drum chosen for the examples is bass drum "1":

Fig. 40 - 2/4

This is a very special snare drum pattern I've learned from my dear friend and great samba master Armando Marçal. The sticking is very characteristic of the samba school Portela, and I recommend that you listen to this samba school in order to recognize this pattern within the *bateria* (drum line):

I believe rudiments are "rhythm codes" that transcend their mere technical aspect. Many times we can recognize a rudimental sticking hidden inside some ancient rhythms from different tribal cultures, especially in hand percussion instruments. Rudiments can be words to be used to express musical speech. You can change the feeling of a rudiment if you sing a specific rhythm cell in the style you want to play. Here is an example I love to use in samba, where I apply the inverted double-stroke roll using the snare drum center and rim shot to create a special feel. It's very important to sing the tamborim figure while you play the snare drum:

Fig. 41 – 2/4 Bass Drum Options

Here is a groove using the snare drum "C" and bass drum "2". Remember, you can create grooves mixing different snare drum patterns and bass drum patterns.

Fig. 42

Groove c + Bass Drum 2

Fig. 43 – 3/4 – The bass drum chosen for these examples is bass drum "1":

Photo: Júlio Cordeiro

An "old fashioned" way of playing the snare drum in Samba is pressing the stick against the head, keeping the pressure throughout every stroke. This was used to keep the volume under control while playing samba in small groups. The sound is unique and percussive, most of the time played with the snares off (*caixa surda*). A great master of this style of playing was Wilson das Neves and also Bezerra da Silva, both of them great composers and percussionists. It's very important to check out their music.

Fig. 44 – 3/4 Bass Drum Options

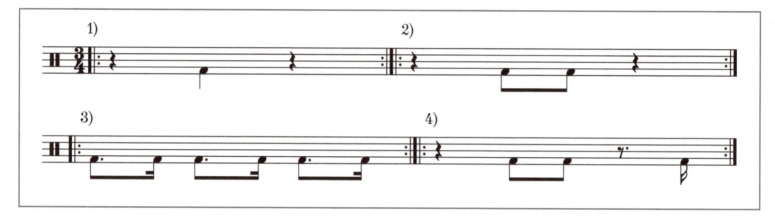

Part 6: Tamborim –
3/4, 5/8, 5/4, 7/8, 7/4, 9/8 and 9/4

Photo: Julio Cordeiro

Part 6: Tamborim

Here is the the tamborim pattern applied in different time signatures in the traditional sense (i.e., played by a dedicated tamborim player with two hands on the instrument):

Fig. 45 – 3/4

Fig. 46 – 5/8

Fig. 47 – 5/4

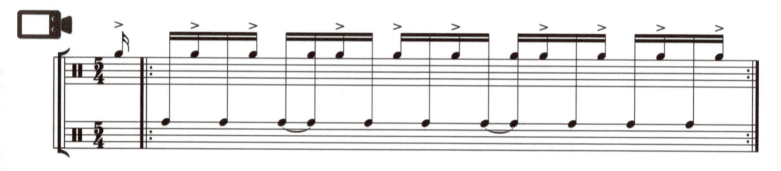

Fig. 48 – 7/8

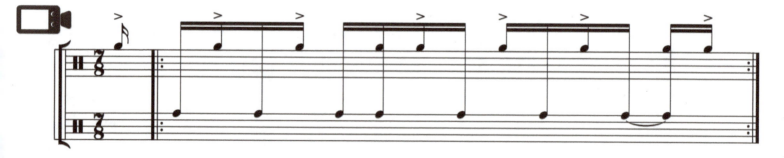

Fig. 49 – 7/4

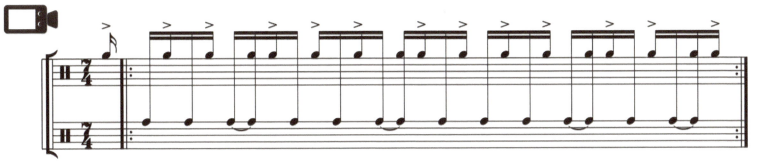

Fig. 50 – 9/8

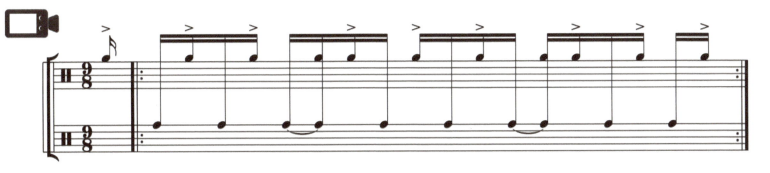

Fig. 51 – 9/4

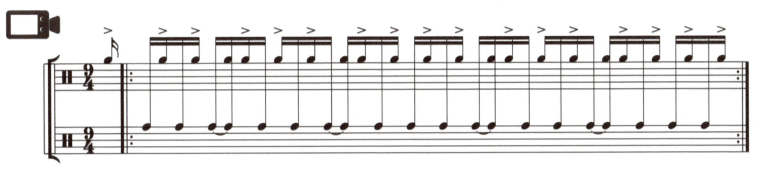

Fig. 52 – 3/4

Part 6: Tamborim

Fig. 53 – 5/84

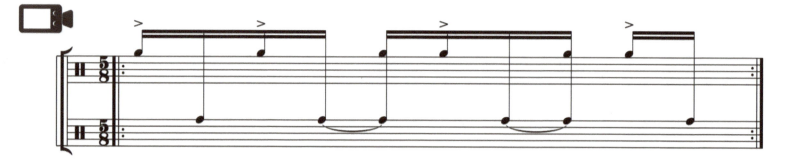

Fig. 54 – 5/4

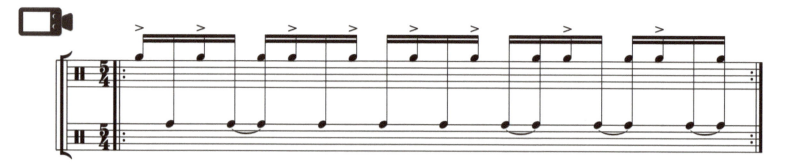

Fig. 55 – 7/8

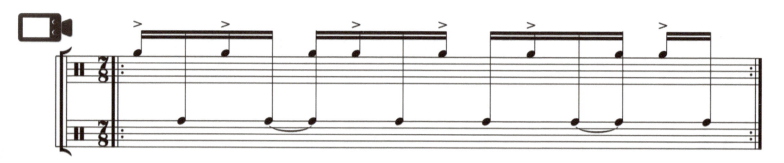

Fig. 56 – 7/4

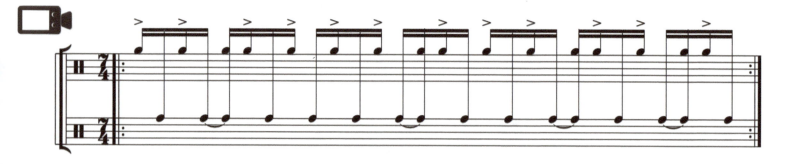

Fig. 57 – 9/8

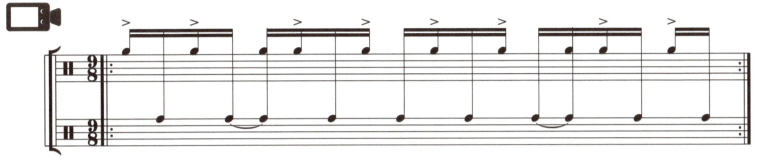

Fig. 58 – 9/4

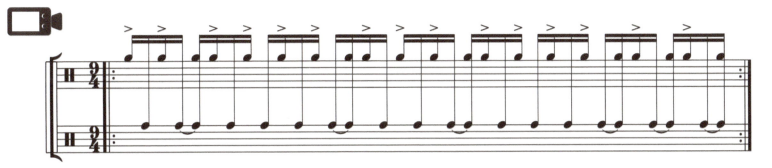

You can create grooves using these tamborim patterns played on the snare drum rim plus 16th notes with the hi-hat, using some of the bass drum examples, or playing the tamborim patterns as a main pulse, using the hi-hat, ride cymbal or cowbell, plus snare and bass drum examples from this book. We will also explore more ideas in the "Odd Time Samba" section of this book.

Photo: Júlio Cordeiro

Part 6: Tamborim

When you play the tamborim in a drum set situation, you play only the main syncopations without the notes played by the finger underneath the tamborim's head, like this:

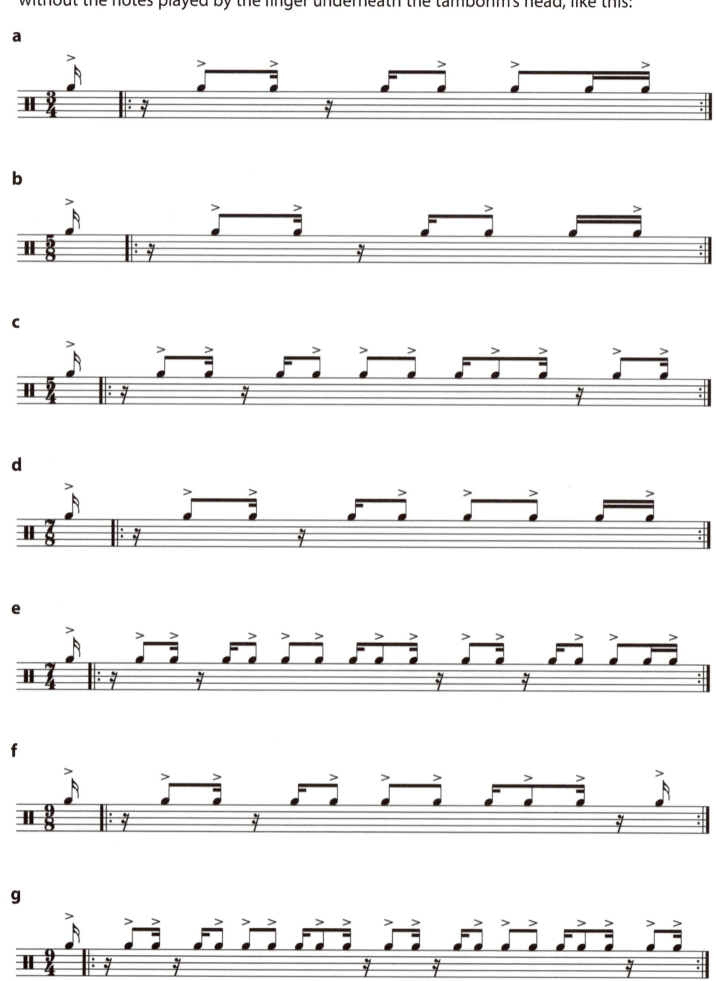

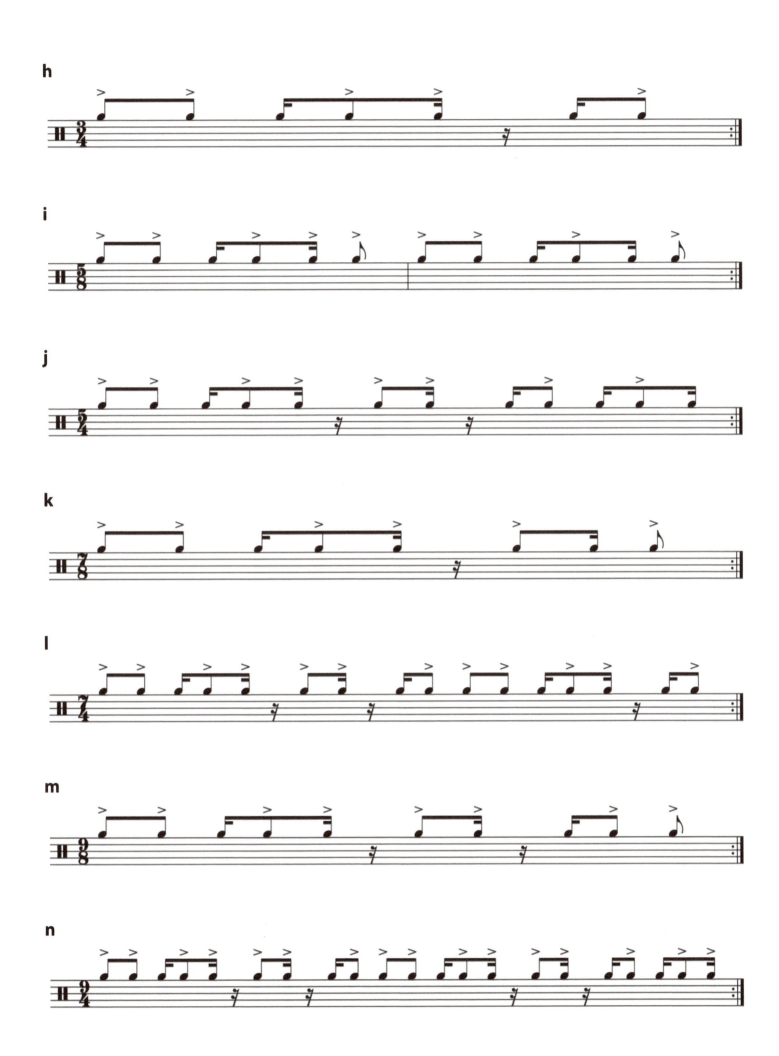

Part 7: Grooves using 16th Notes

Photo: Júlio Cordeiro

When the Brazilian styles, like samba, were first adapted to the drum set, the drummers would play mainly the snare drum, bass drum and toms to emulate the traditional rhythms. Later (especially after the birth of bossa nova), drummers started to use the cymbals to keep the time and feel.

Here are some samba examples with the sixteenth-note pulse played by the lead hand. In these examples the idea is to keep your right hand (left hand if you are lefthanded) playing sixteenth notes all the time, while you play the other combinations with the left hand (right hand if you are left-handed).

Fig. 59

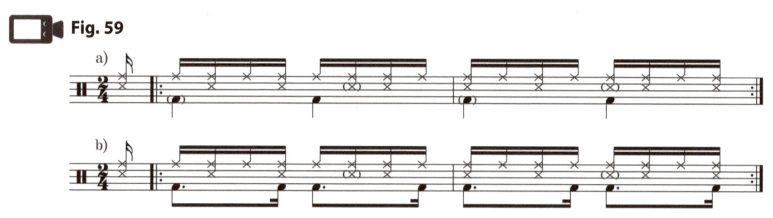

Use the above drum variations.

Fig. 60

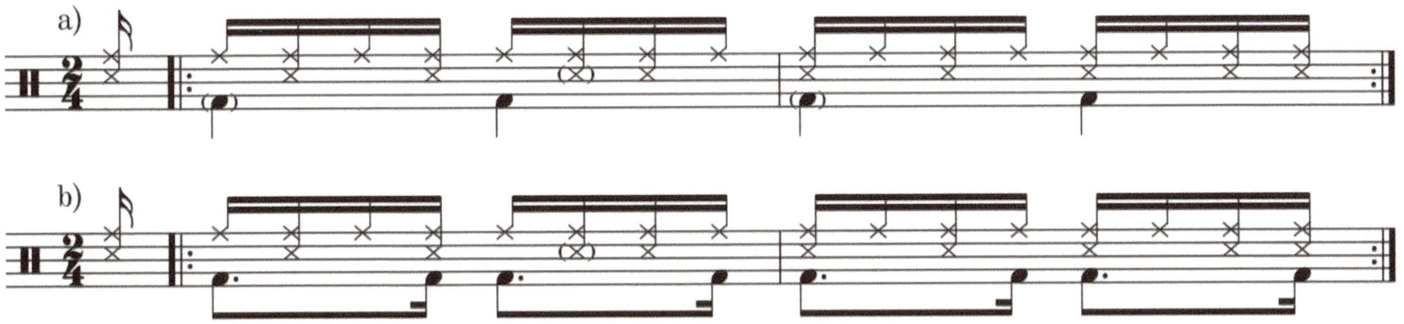

a)

b)

Fig. 61

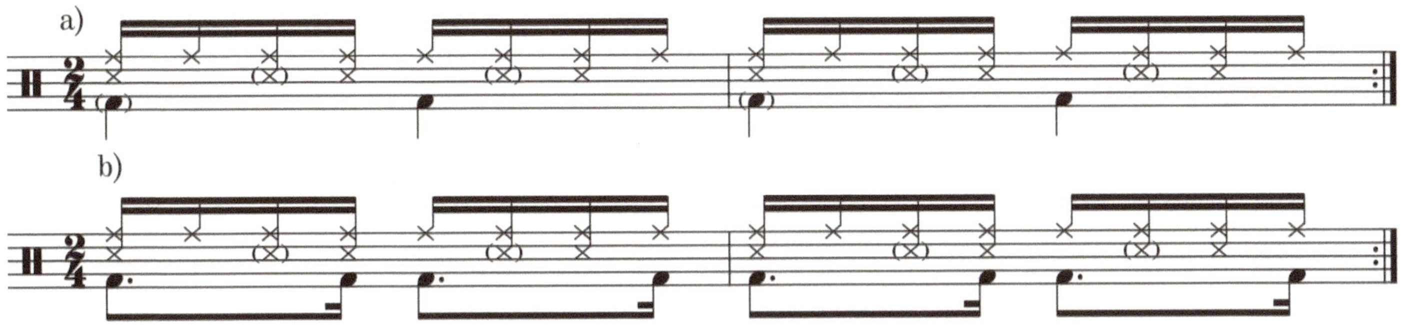

a)

b)

Fig. 62

a)

b)

Fig. 63

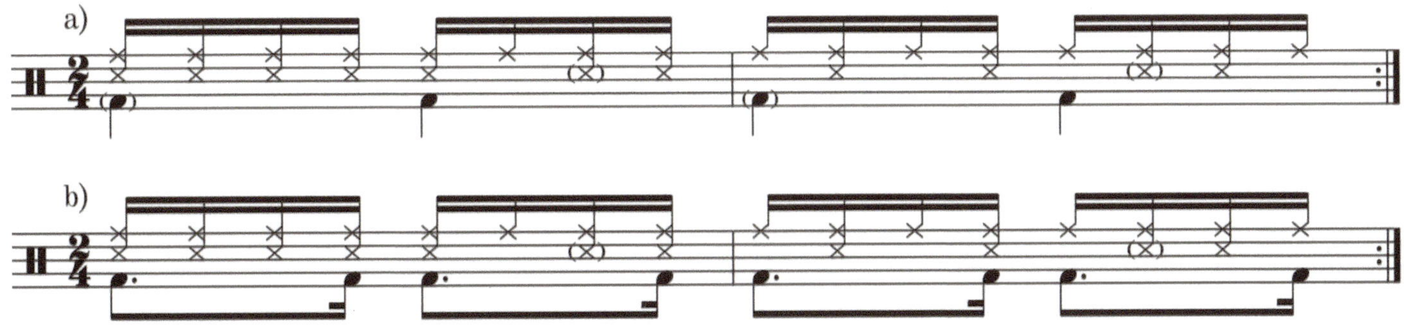

a)

b)

Part 7: Grooves using 16th Notes

Fig. 64

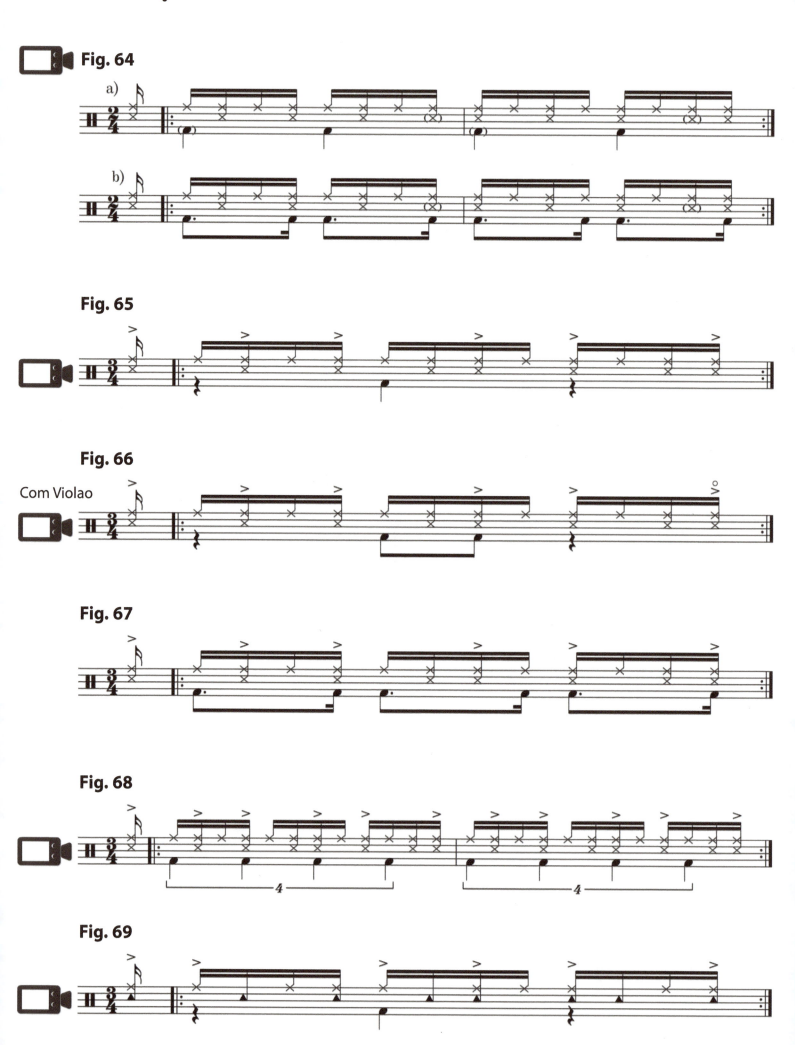

Fig. 65

Fig. 66

Com Violao

Fig. 67

Fig. 68

Fig. 69

Bossa Nova

The next examples use sixteenth notes on the hi-hat or ride cymbal in a bossa nova context. Everything is played softly, and the rim of the snare drum plays a minimalist variation of the tamborim (figures based on João Gilberto's guitar playing), with the patterns starting mainly on the downbeat.

It is very important to listen to albums like João Gilberto's Chega de Saudade, Elizeth Cardoso's *Canção do Amor Demais* and Tom Jobim's *Tide and Wave*, in order to absorb the sound and aesthetic of the style. Drummers like Juquinha Stockler, Milton Banana, João Palma, Edison Machado, Dom Um Romão, and the percussionist Guarany Nogueira were very important innovators of bossa nova drumming.

Fig. 70

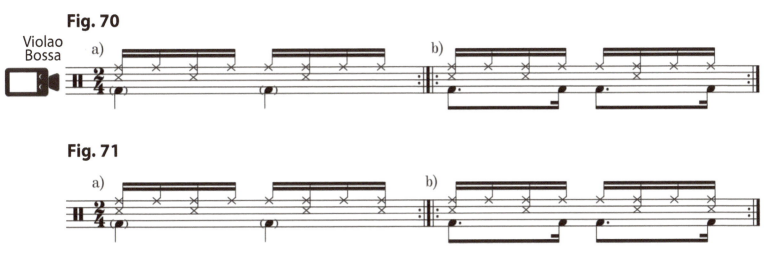

Fig. 71

It is possible to create a softer color when we use one brush playing the hi-hat plus the stick playing the snare rim, like this:

Fig. 72– Right Hand – Brushes

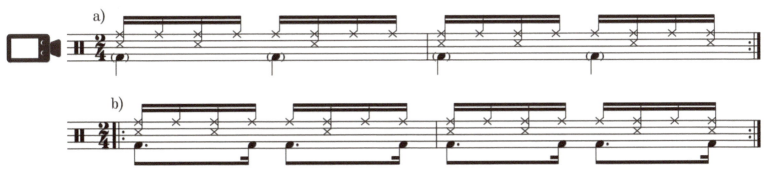

Fig. 73

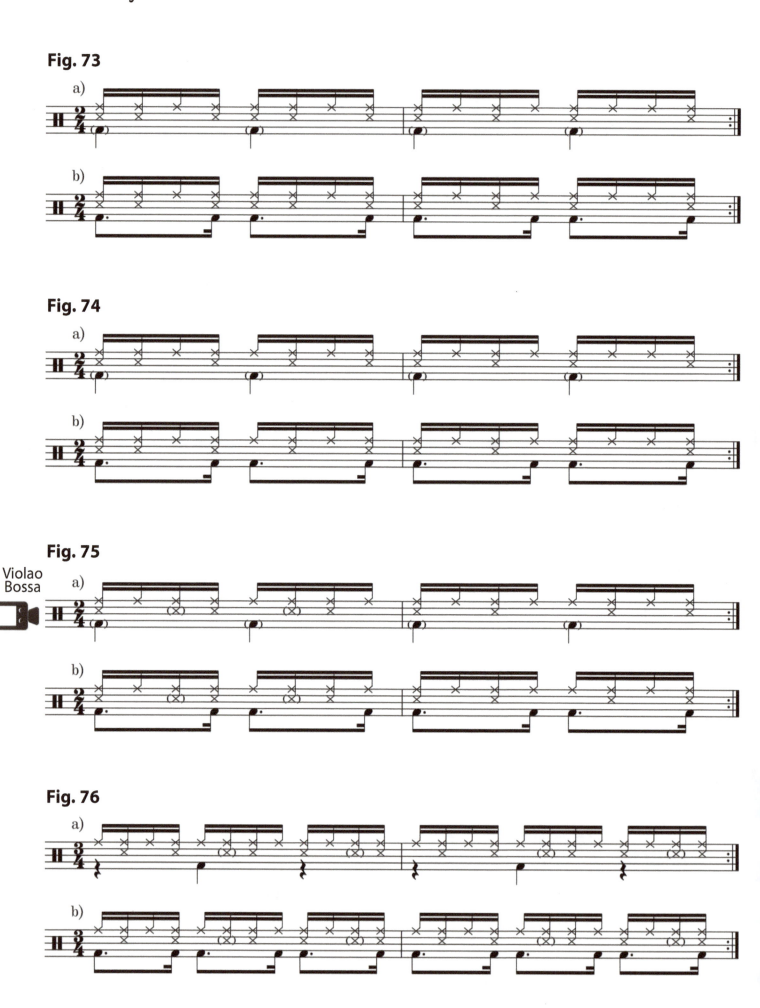

Fig. 74

Fig. 75

Violao
Bossa

Fig. 76

Adding the tamborim, it is possible to have very beautiful and soft colors in the groove:

Fig. 77

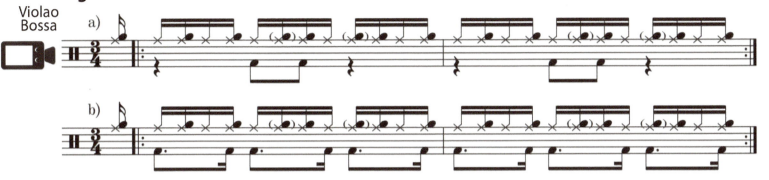

Partido Alto

Partido alto is a samba style with a very specific figure and accent, played originally on the *pandeiro*. Here is the complete pattern:

Fig. 78

In my drum set adaptation, I omit the downbeat in the beginning of the second bar of the groove, to give more fluidity, like this:

Fig. 79

I find it very interesting to keep the tamborim figure going on independently, using the hi-hat, ride cymbal or cowbell. It's very important to sing the bass drum/snare drum combination while you play the tamborim pattern on the hi-hat:

Fig. 80

Fig. 80a

Here is an interesting example of partido alto in 9/8, respecting the tamborim pattern and the partido alto pattern:

Fig. 81

Samba Funk

Mixing the tamborim pattern with some backbeats and sixteenth notes combinations can create some nice, funky grooves. Practice all four sixteenth notes independently on the bass drum and snare drum, with the tamborim pattern played on the hi-hat, in order to feel comfortable with the coordination when creating grooves.

For the following examples, keep the tamborim figure on the hi-hat:

Fig. 82

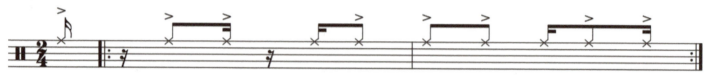

Fig. 83

Fig. 84

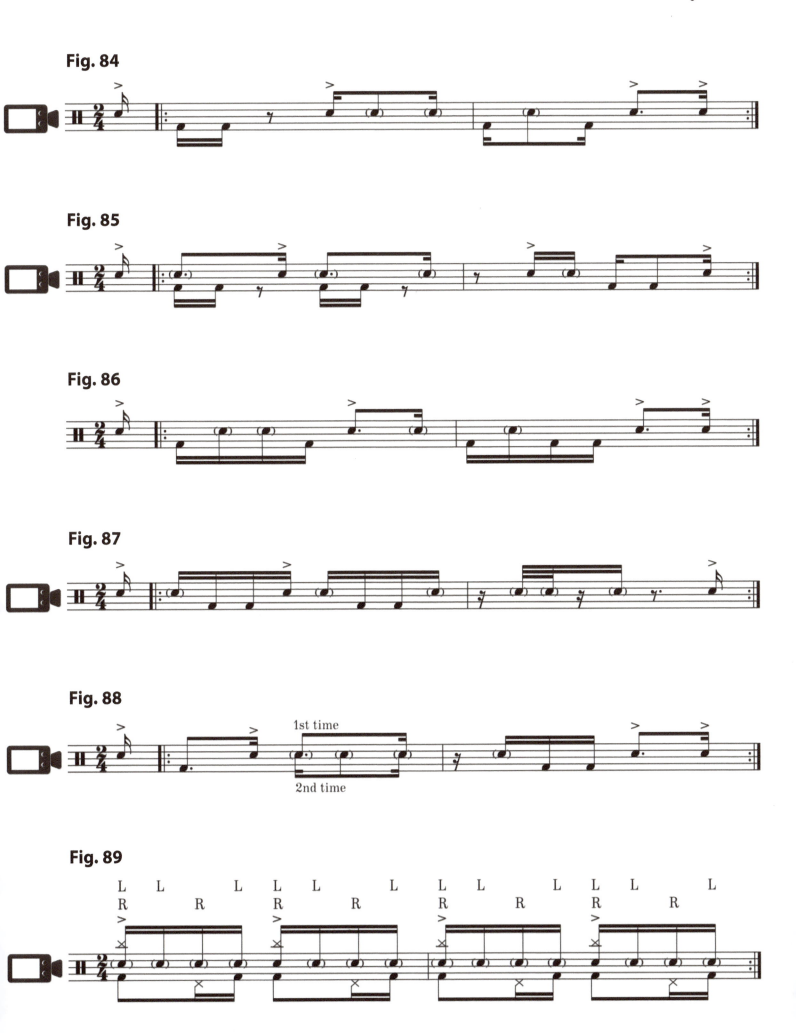

Fig. 85

Fig. 86

Fig. 87

Fig. 88

Fig. 89

To have more punch and different colors in the groove, sometimes I play the hi-hat and snare drum in unison, using the tip of the stick on the hi-hat and the end of the stick on the snare drum, like this:

Fig. 90

Fig. 91

Photo: Júlio Cordeiro

Part 8: Brushes I

There are many ways of using the brushes to play samba. I like to start with the use of small circular movements with both hands, creating a figure like this:

Fig. 92

EXPLAIN

• STARTING POINT

▼ BRUSH DIRECTION

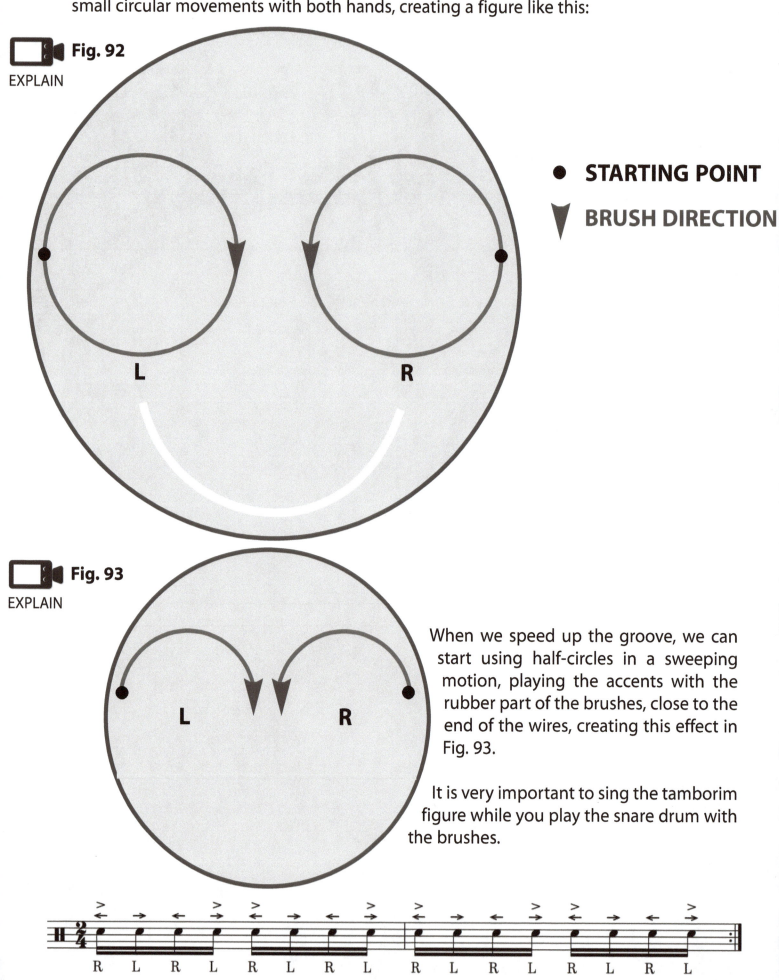

Fig. 93

EXPLAIN

When we speed up the groove, we can start using half-circles in a sweeping motion, playing the accents with the rubber part of the brushes, close to the end of the wires, creating this effect in Fig. 93.

It is very important to sing the tamborim figure while you play the snare drum with the brushes.

Adding the bass drum, we can play the second surdo, keeping the beater of the pedal in contact with the head, playing very softly and with heel up technique; and the first surdo, removing the beater of the head and playing a little harder using a heel down technique, in a kind of up stroke/down stroke motion (remembering that this works better in a bass drum without a hole, so you have a fuller sounding bass drum). This is explained in the example before Figure 19.

Fig. 94

Now we'll add the hi-hat with the left foot, playing closed and opened sounds, generating a nice movement to the groove:

Fig. 95

Using a hybrid concept, I like to play a circle with the left hand in a sweeping motion (sometimes playing some accents on the second sixteenth notes, sometimes just accentuating the "e" part of the beat) and taps with the right hand, playing the first, third, and fourth sixteenth notes, starting a linear trajectory from the bottom of the snare drum for the first tap, going up for the second tap and coming down for the third tap, closer to the starting point, where the figure starts again, like this:

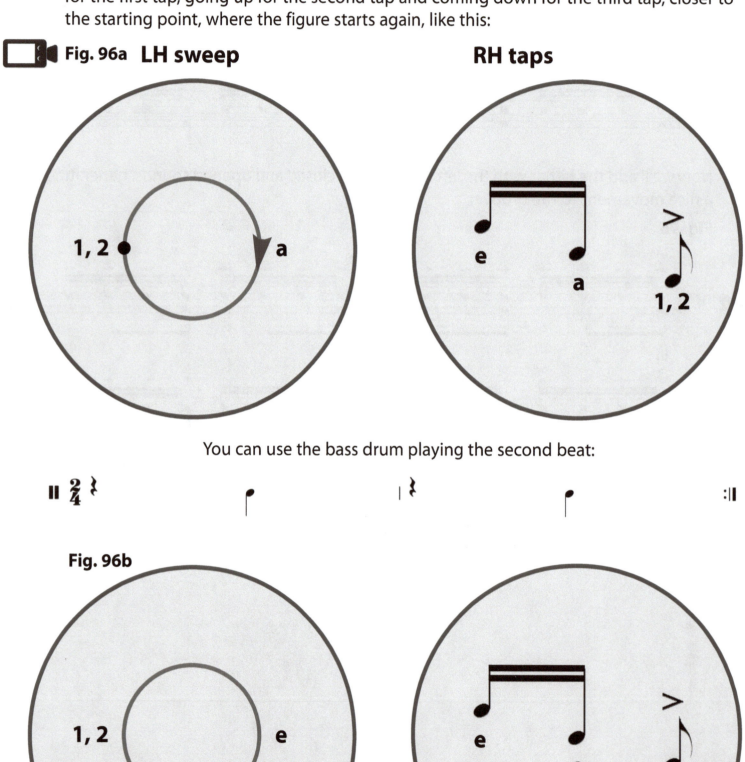

Fig. 96a LH sweep

RH taps

You can use the bass drum playing the second beat:

Fig. 96b

Written in the traditional snare drum notation, we have a figure like this:

Fig. 96 a

The half-circle above the second sixteenth note is the same sweeping motion in the previous graphic. Always remember to sing the tamborim pattern while you play these examples.

Adding the bass drum and hi-hat, we have a very interesting groove that works great in medium and fast tempos using the brushes:

Fig. 97 a

Fig. 97 b

Again using the small circles in sweeping motion, I have an interesting way of playing the *choro* on the drum set. Playing the first and the third sixteenth notes with the right hand very softly (with a little accent on the first note), and the second and fourth sixteenth notes with the left hand, we have a sound texture very similar to the pandeiro, like this:

Fig. 98

Bass drum and hi-hat combinations:

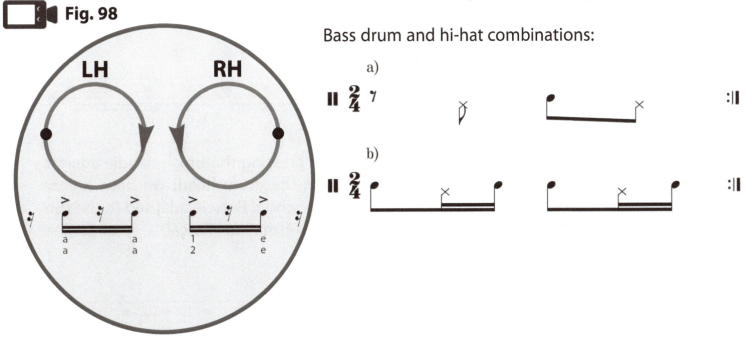

For slow sambas and samba-canção, I also use a groove where I play a long sweep motion with the right hand. It is shaped like a letter "L" starting on the top-right part of the snare drum for the first sixteenth note and ending on the bottom-right part of the snare corresponding to the third sixteenth note ("e"), while I play a long circle with the left hand with a little accent on the fourth sixteenth note:

Fig. 99

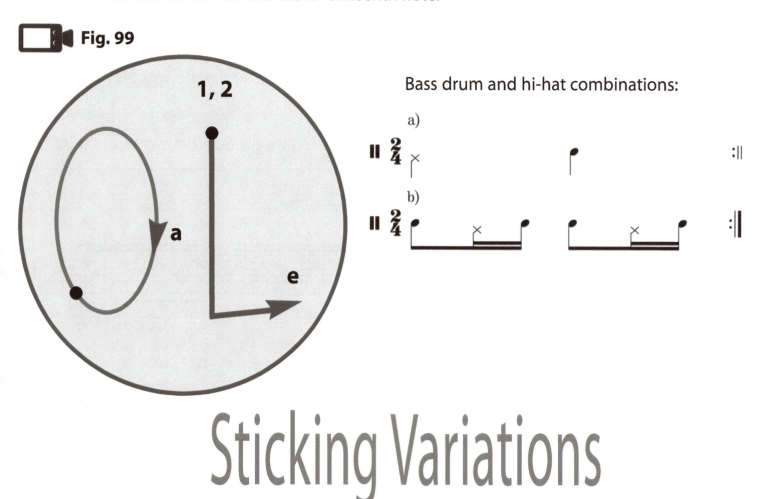

Bass drum and hi-hat combinations:

Sticking Variations

Using different sticking variations, you can use upstroke and downstroke movements in order to get a more fluent groove. Normally I play this groove on a typical samba snare drum (the snare drum they play in the samba schools):

Fig. 100

Using the rebound of the wires of the brush (slightly pressing the brush handle against the rim of the snare and letting it bounce freely on the drum head) we have a very traditional snare drum samba pattern from the samba school Portela adapted to the use of the brushes. I learned this pattern with my friend Armando Marçal, a great samba master. Here it is:

Fig. 101

You can choose which bass drum/hi-hat pattern you want to play depending on the feel required for the song. The first pattern has a little bit more of a laid-back feel, while the second example has a forward motion, moving the music ahead:

Fig. 101a – Bass Drum and Hi-Hat Options:

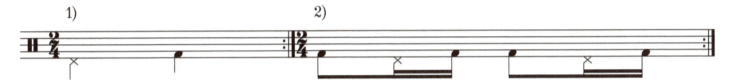

Part 9: Samba School Adaptation

Inside the heart of this little boy from Portela beats the samba.

To have a samba school flavor, I use this sticking: L L R L L L R L and play the first sixteenth note of each beat on a low tom. This sticking creates a surdo feel while the snare drum still plays all four sixteenth notes.

Fig. 102 a

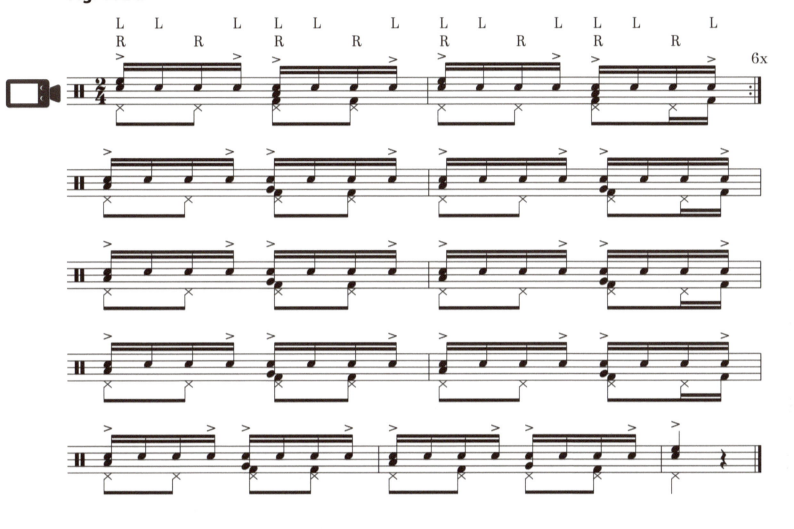

Fig. 102 b

A great-sounding option is to have the same pattern above played on the tamborim, accenting the first sixteenth note of each beat on the ride cymbal (especially one with rivets). This creates a tamborim ensemble feel:

Fig. 103

Samba / Funk - Brushes

We can also play some very interesting, funky samba grooves using the brushes. When I add the backbeat to the groove, I use a sideways movement and play with the beginning of the rubber handle of the brush, to have more of a staccato sound:

Fig. 104

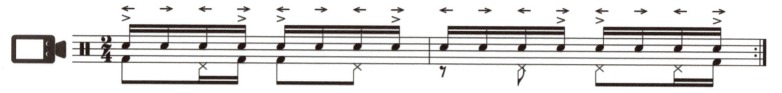

Fig. Fig. 104a – Bass Drum Option:

You can also play a funkier version with the circular motion, like this:

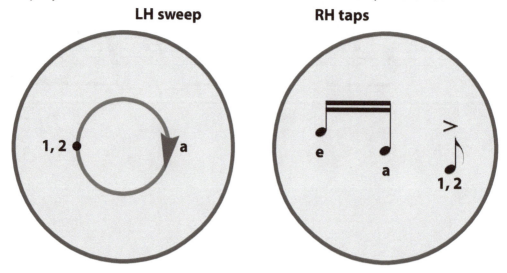

It is very important to keep the child alive inside yourself. What inspired you to begin playing? Where is the joy and sparkling fire of that dream?

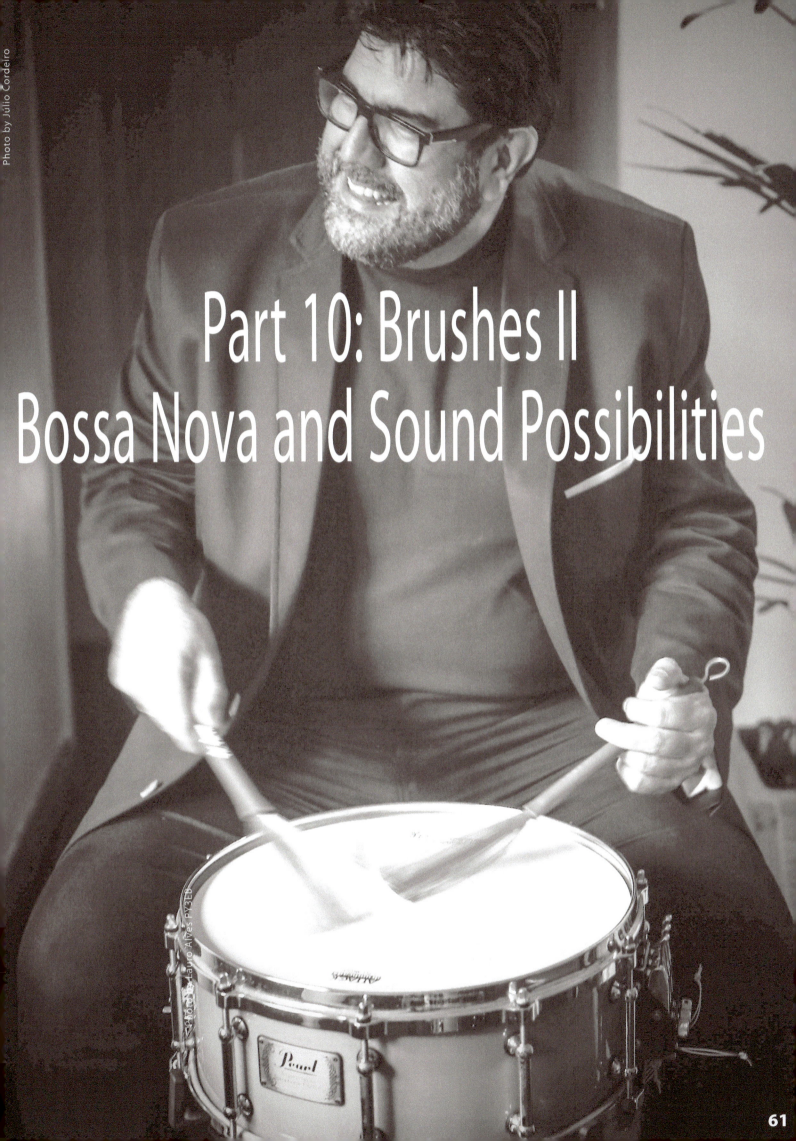

Part 10: Brushes II
Bossa Nova and Sound Possibilities

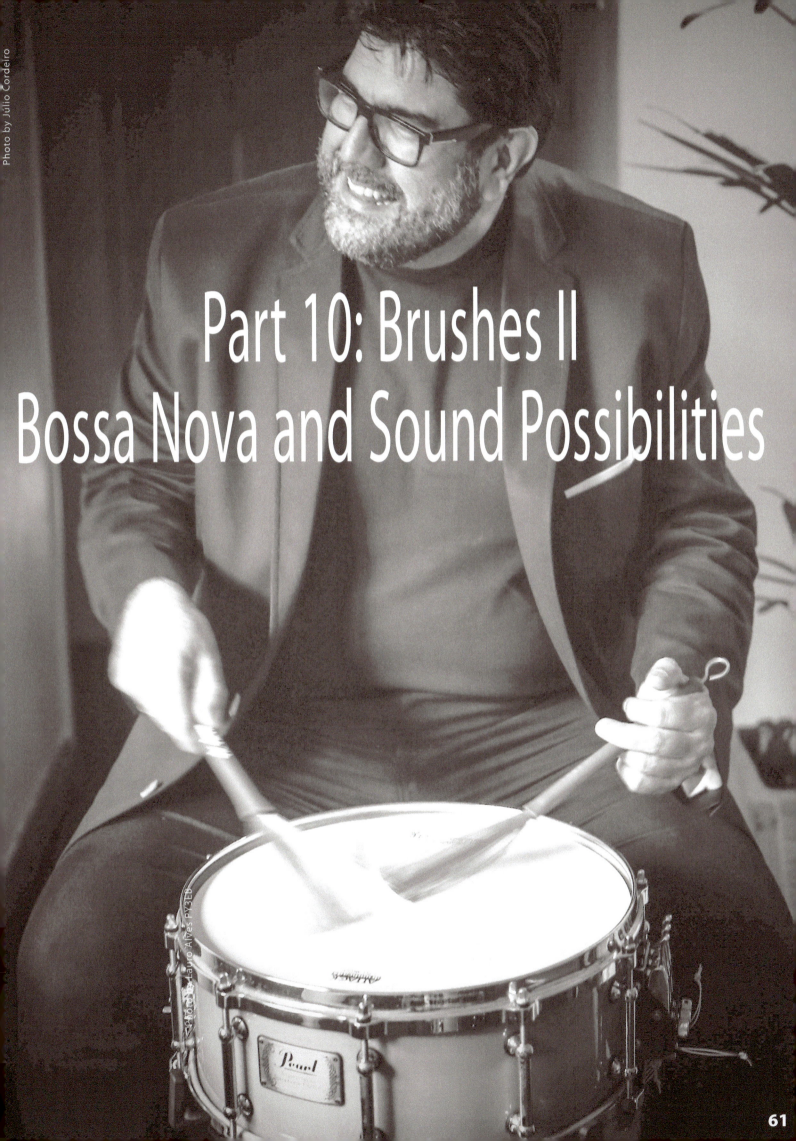

The universe of bossa nova is much softer, sensitive and minimalist than samba. The colors of bossa nova are less bright, with darker tonalities. The great João Bosco always says, "Bossa nova has a special light. It is not that bright and solar light of Dorival Caymmi, but it's not the dark and rainy light of Noel Rosa."

João Gilberto, with his special voice and unique interpretation, has created the master-groove of bossa nova on his guitar. In order to understand and feel this very important style of music, it is almost obligatory to listen to the album *Chega de Saudade*, recorded by Gilberto in 1959 and considered bossa nova's seminal work. On many great records of the bossa nova era, drummers played the brushes on a phone book, in order to have an even softer and more subtle sound!

Here we have an application of the brushes in the bossa nova. The left hand plays circles in sweeping motion starting on the left side of the snare drum towards the center of the drum, playing little accents on the two eighth notes of each beat. The right hand plays taps, very softly, emulating João Gilberto's guitar pattern. The bass drum plays only quarter notes (also very softly).

Fig. 105

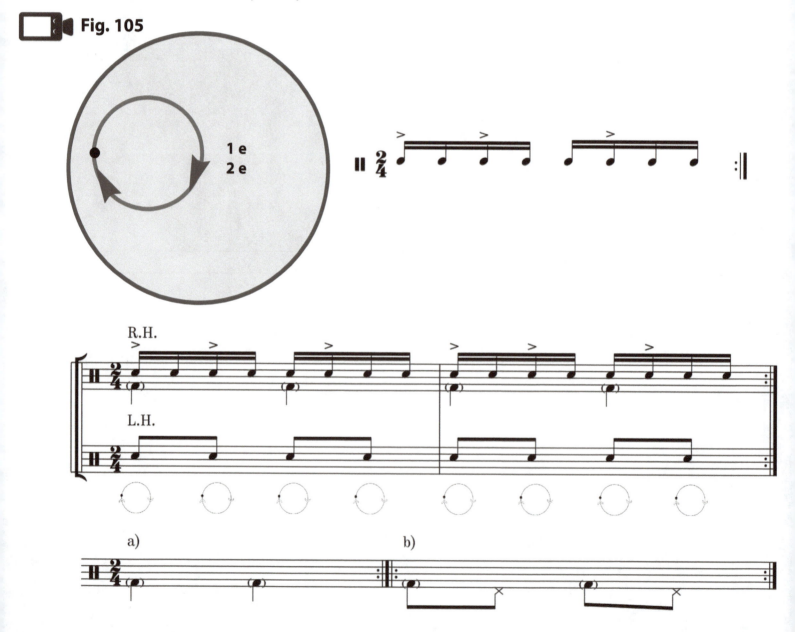

Adding the hi-hat playing on the second eighth note of each beat, we have a very basic and effective bossa nova groove:

Fig. 106

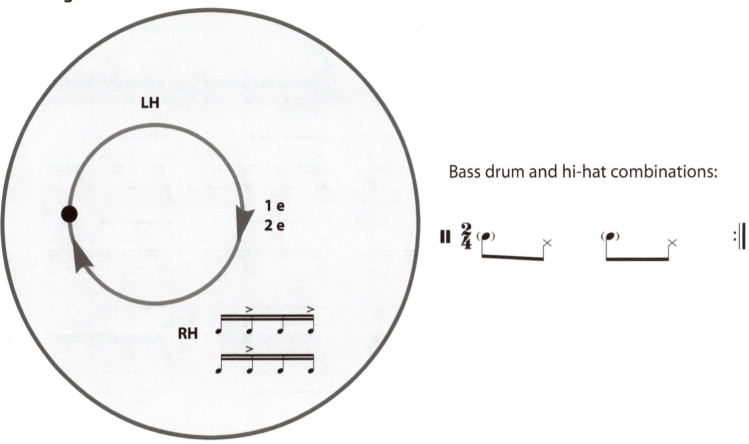

Bass drum and hi-hat combinations:

To create a softer version, slightly changing the color of sounds, we can use a sweeping motion with the right hand, playing sixteenth notes or thirty-second notes on the snare drum, plus the left hand playing the classic bossa nova pattern—with the brush—on the hi-hat:

Fig. 107

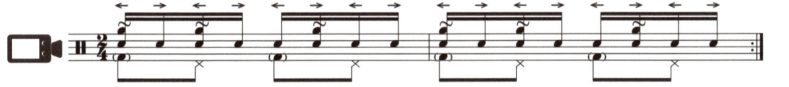

Fig. 108

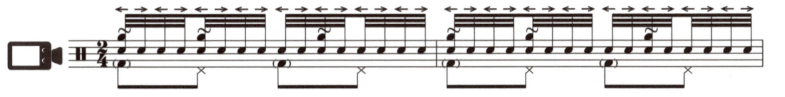

In a musical situation, you can mix the two examples above, creating new colors inside the tune.

It is also very nice to create new colors by using the hands combined with the brushes, sticks, or mallets. Here is an example of mixing the sweeping motion of the brushes with the right hand and the left hand playing on the snare drum, with everything played very softly, in the bossa nova atmosphere:

 **Fig. 109**

To have a little more punch in the groove, I play the hi-hat with the left hand (using the brush), while the right hand plays the snare drum in a "sideways" motion, using a kind of tap mixed with the sweeping motion:

Fig. 110

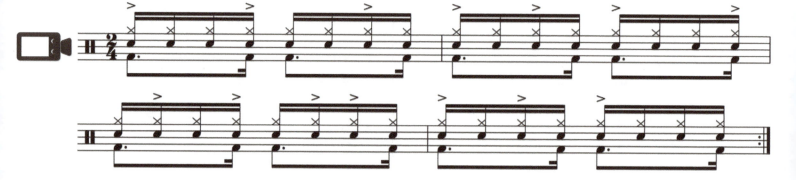

Part 11: Odd Time Samba Grooves

5/8

5/4

7/8

7/4

9/8

9/4

Photo by Júlio Cordeiro

In a contemporary context, many Brazilian styles were adapted by great composers using odd time signatures. Writers like Hermeto Pascoal, Airto Moreira, Nenê, Egberto Gismonti, Milton Nascimento, João Bosco, and many others used different time signatures in their compositions.

Here I will show some examples of my own creation that I like to use when I play samba in odd time. I will give examples of grooves keeping steady sixteenth notes on the hi-hat or ride cymbal (a post-bossa nova approach) and also examples where I try to respect the tamborim pattern as an independent voice while I play the snare drum and bass drum (a more percussive approach).

Always remember to sing each part of the groove while you play and feel the tamborim. Always count, too!

It is very important to keep in mind the "question-and-answer" aspect of the tamborim rhythm. For example, we will feel the 5/8 samba in a "question" in 3 and an "answer" in 2. Remember to count out this 3:2 pulse while you play the tamborim pattern and the whole groove.

5/8 Grooves

In the following examples, the tamborim pattern will be played on the cowbell using the snare drum cross-stick (playing in the position of the snare rim, but with the tip of the stick playing the cowbell), while we keep the right hand (left hand if you are lefthanded) playing constant sixteenth notes on the hi-hat. The bass drum will change in each example, giving a different pulse to the groove:

Fig. 111

Fig. 112

Fig. 113

Fig. 114

Fig. 115

In the next two examples the tamborim pattern will be played on the hi-hat, driving the samba groove with a more percussive flavor.

Fig. 116

Here, I play a 5/4 idea on the bass drum over two measures of 5/8, creating a polyrhythmic idea:

Fig. 117

Here is a snare drum pattern to create the samba school/batucada feel in the 5/8 groove:

Fig. 118

Next we have a small batucada in 5/8. Always remember to sing the tamborim rhythm while you play, internalizing the feel.

Fig. 119

Fig. 120

You can also use the following bass drum/hi-hat variation:
Fig. 121

5/4 Grooves

Fig. 122

Fig. 123

Fig. 124

Fig. 125 a

Here is a version of this groove with the bass drum going over bar line, creating a hypnotic feeling that resolves after 3 bars:

Fig. 125 b

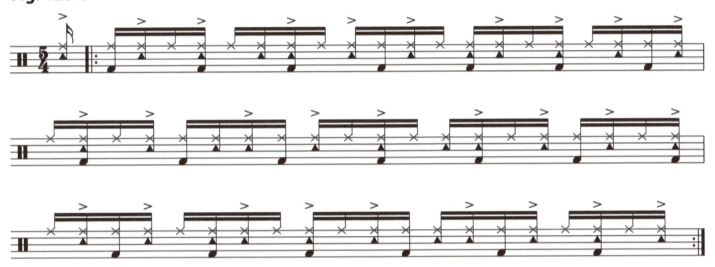

Fig. 126

Fig. 127

Fig. 128

7/8 Grooves

Here is the question-and-answer feel of the tamborim in the 7/8 groove. The question is a 4 pulse and the answer is a 3 pulse:

Fig. 129

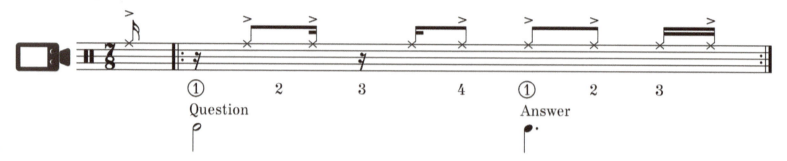

Fig. 130

Fig. 131

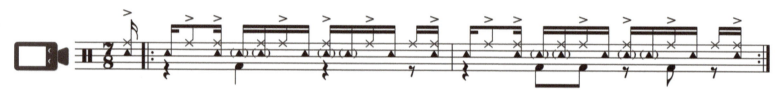

Here are some snare drum patterns to internalize the samba school/batucada feel in 7/8. It is very important to sing the tamborim pattern to make these snare drum figures sound natural.

Fig. 132

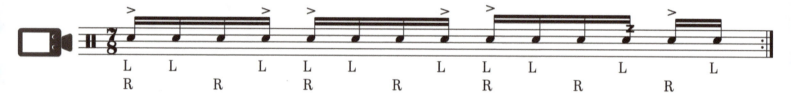

Fig. 133

In this example, I lead with my right hand, using the tamborim "voice" to generate the feel:

Fig. 134

After you feel comfortable with the snare drum patterns, you can add the bass drum. Here are some examples you can mix with the snare drum patterns:
Fig. 135 (Fig. 134 with Bass Drum 136a)

Fig. 135 (Fig. 134 with Bass Drum 136a)

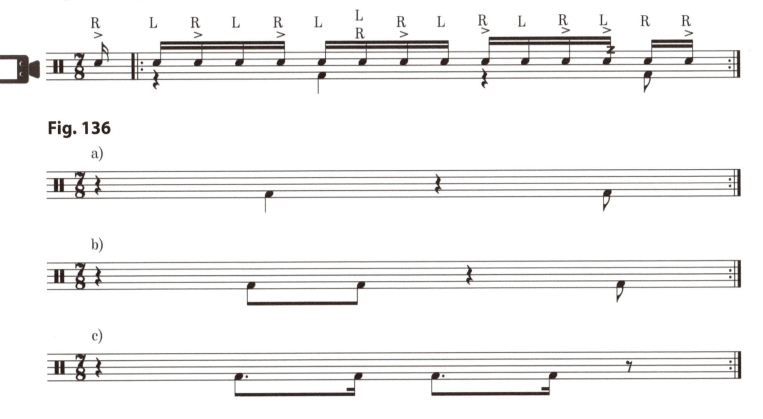

Fig. 136

Here is a full batucada example in 7/8:

Fig. 137

Fig. 138

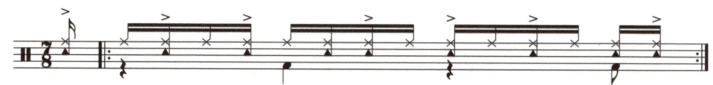

Fig. 139

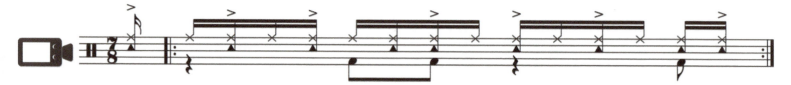

Fig. 140

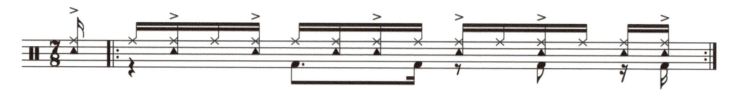

Fig. 141

7/4 Grooves

Here are some grooves in 7/4 using constant sixteenth notes played on the hi-hat. The tamborim rhythms are played on the snare rim with the cross-stick.

Fig. 142

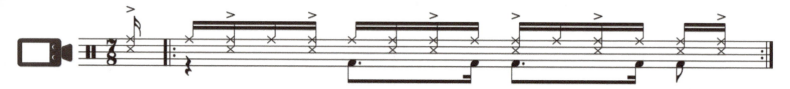

Fig. 143

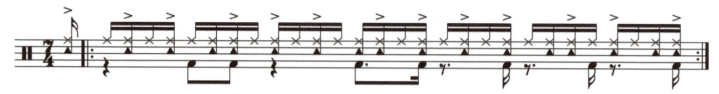

Fig. 144

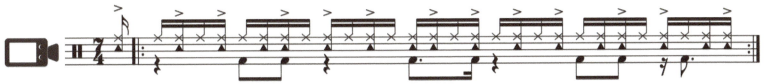

Fig. 145

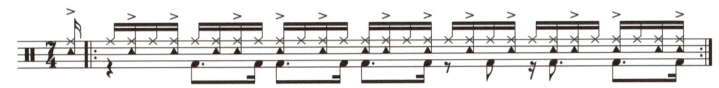

Here is an example of the samba snare drum adapted to the 7/4 groove. It is very important to sing the tamborim pattern in 7/4 while you play this:

Fig. 146

Here I use the tamborim pattern in 7/4 as the main pulse, instead of playing all the sixteenth notes on the hi-hat:

Fig. 147

Here is a transcription of Hermeto Pascoal's "Música das Nuvens e do Chão" (from the album *Cérebro Magnético*) basic groove, to give you an example of a different approach to the 7/4 samba feel:

Fig. 148

Here is my adaptation using the tamborim pattern played on the hi-hat. Pay attention to how the tamborim pattern starts: this time it starts on the downbeat to match the melody of the song:

Fig. 149

Fig. 150

9/8 Grooves

As we learned earlier, it is very important to feel the question-and-answer aspect of the samba rhythm when playing in odd time signatures. Here you can see the 9/8 groove (tamborim pattern) in two groups: one of 4 pulses and one of 5 pulses. Notice the "question" part starts syncopated, with one sixteenth note before beat 1, while the "answer" part starts on beat 1 of the 5 pulse. Sing out the 4 and 5 pulses while you play the tamborim pattern.

Fig. 151

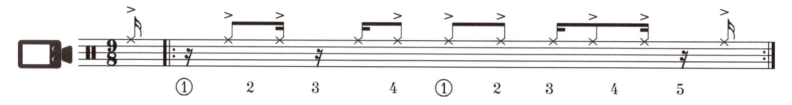

Fig. 152

Fig. 153

You can add different colors to the groove above by playing the right hand on the tamborim, adding the hi-hat, rim shots and so on.

Fig. 154

Fig. 155

9/4 Grooves

Here we have some grooves with the tamborim pattern played on the snare drum rim, while the right hand (left hand if you are left-handed) plays sixteenth notes on the hi-hat:

Fig. 156

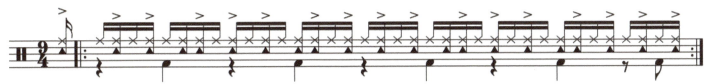

Fig. 157

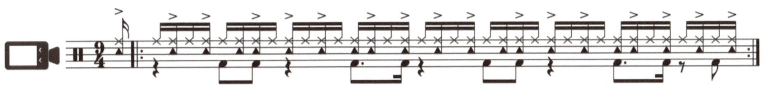

Here's a version with a slightly different tamborim pattern:

Fig. 158

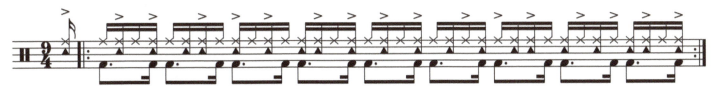

In this example in 9/4, I divide the bass drum into three groups of quarter notes and add a four-over-three pulse over each group. This will create a 12-over-9 feel in the bass drum. I play constant sixteenth notes on the hi-hat and the tamborim figure on the snare drum rim:

Fig. 159

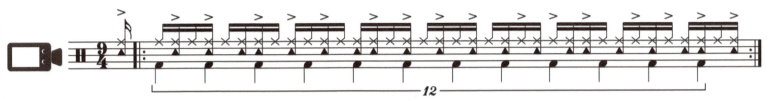

Part 11: Odd Time Samba Grooves

Fig. 160

Fig. 161

Photo by Júlio Cordeiro

Part 12: Rhythmic Words

I like to feel the rhythm generated by the groups of subdivisions as "words" that can create phrases when internalized and put together.

I like to feel the rhythm generated by the groups of subdivisions as "words" that can create phrases when internalized and put together. In a contemporary context, I use these rhythmic groups as words to organize new grooves and phrases:

Fig. 162

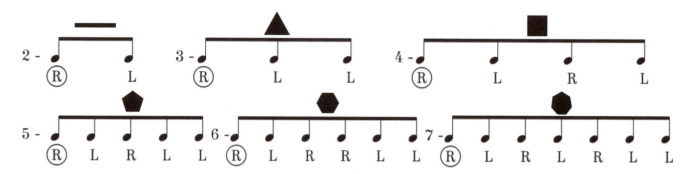

It is important to practice each rhythmic word with different subdivisions, like the "word" 3 (RLL) practiced in 4 subdivisions per tempo (sixteenth notes if we are in 3/4):

Fig. 163

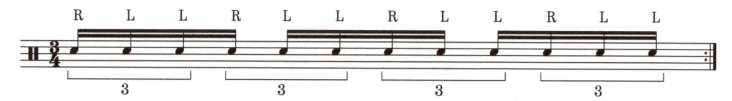

The Brazilian rhythm *marcha* can be felt as a 3-3-3-3-4 phrase in a 4/4 measure. We have 16 sixteenth notes in this measure (4 per beat), so if I group them in the words 3-3-3-3-4, I will have this phrase:

Fig. 164

After you feel comfortable with the rhythmic words in many subdivisions, you can apply them in the samba groove, creating new pulses inside the beat. Here is a 3/4 samba groove where we have 12 sixteenth notes per measure. To create an interesting phrase, we can group the rhythmic words in 3-2-2-5 over the samba bass drum and hi-hat, like this:

Fig. 165

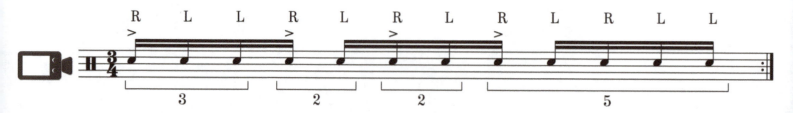

Fig. 166

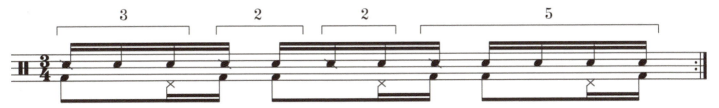

Then we can add some different colors using the cowbells, toms, and snare drum, giving the phrase a Brazilian accent:

Fig. 167

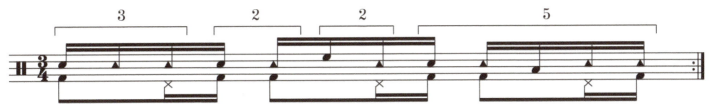

Here is another way of creating a phrase using the rhythmic words 3-4-5 in the 3/4 samba:

Fig. 168

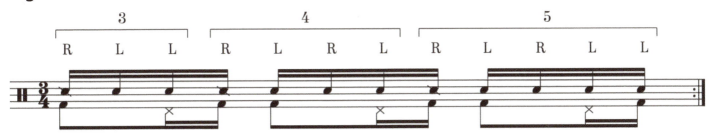

Adding the toms and snare drum mixed with the cowbell, we have a very Afro/Brazilian phrase and groove. Listen to the tune "Cravo e Canela," by the great Milton Nascimento, where you can find a feel very close to the 3-4-5 phrase in the A section melody.

Fig. 169

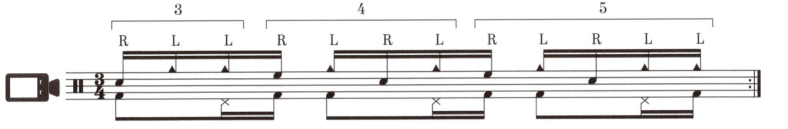

I like to use the concept of the rhythmic words in a broader context. Instead of grouping subdivisions, I start to make groups of beats/pulses inside the measure, creating a "meter within a meter."

For example, if we have two bars of 4/4, we will have 8 pulses of quarter notes:

Fig. 170

Now, if I want to create a 3/4 pulse over this 4/4 form, I can have 2 groups of 3 quarter notes and one group of 2 quarter notes:

Fig. 171

Then I will use the tamborim pattern in 3/4 two times (played on the snare drum rim) and complete the samba feel in the last two quarter notes of the measure (also using the snare drum rim). This is accompanied with steady sixteenth notes on the hi-hat. This is a very nice way of phrasing inside the samba style:

Fig. 172 a

Fig. 172 b

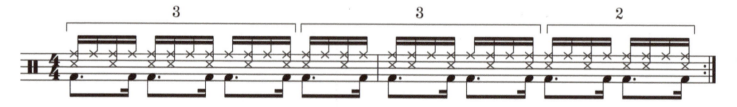

Here is a "5¼" phrasing idea. When I expand this idea to a form of 4 bars in 4/4 (16 quarter-note pulses) I can have 5 groups of 3 quarter notes plus 1 quarter note:

Fig. 173 a

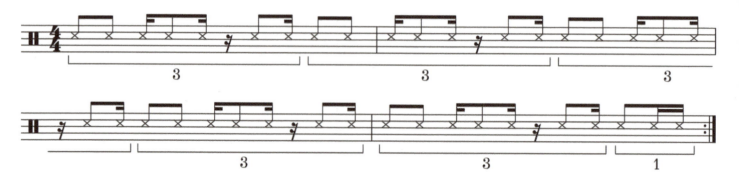

Then I add the whole 3/4 samba idea to create a different pulse inside the groove:

Fig. 173 b

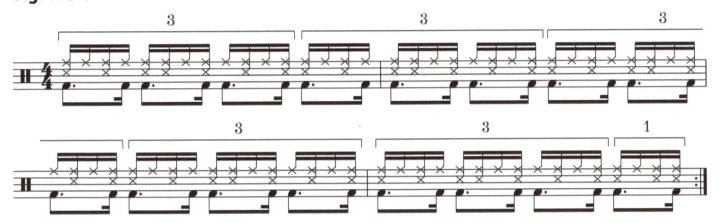

Now, to add more complexity to the groove and phrasing, I can add 4 quarter notes on the bass drum over each one of the 5 pulses of 3/4 samba (creating a 4-against-3 pulse, 5 times over the 4/4 form):

Fig. 173 c

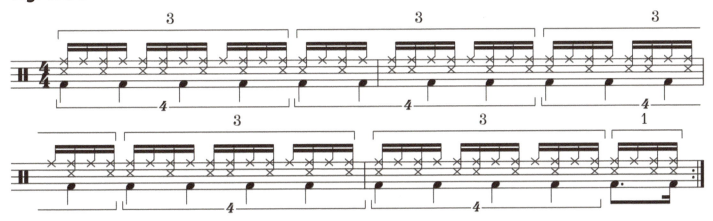

It's also possible to create a new meteric pattern of 5-3 over the two bars of 4/4, like this:

Fig. 174 a

Here is the tamborim phrase in the 5-3 pulse:

Fig. 174 b

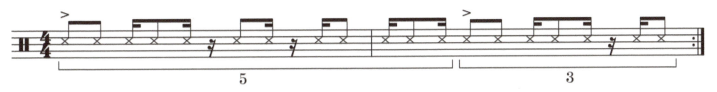

Here I will use a 5-3 tamborim phrase in a two-bar 4/4 form (8 quarter note pulses), creating a longer motive to the groove:

Fig. 174 c

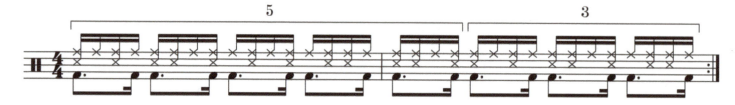

Here is an example of a groove in 11/16, where the pulse is 4-4-3. Remember to be creative and explore the colors of the set when you feel comfortable with the pulse and the rhythmic words.

Fig. 175 a

Fig. 175 b

Fig. 176

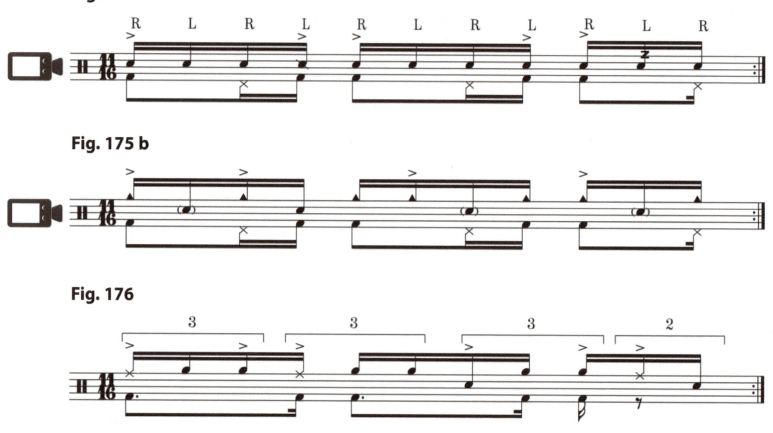

Samba groove in 7/8, using the rhythmic words 5-5-4:

Fig. 177

Here is a groove in 15/16 with the phrase 5-5-5, keeping the samba atmosphere:

Fig. 178

And here is a groove in 13/16 using the phrase 4-4-5, with the tamborim played on the snare drum and the hi-hat keeping the sixteenth notes:

Fig. 179

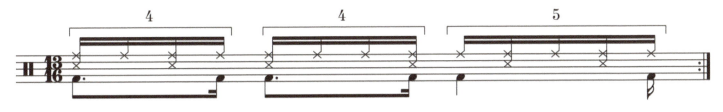

"Kiko's applications of Brazilian rhythms to drum set are only a matter of pure musicianship—yet if they are full of technical difficulties it is only in service of the music. So this is not another Brazilian rhythms drum book, this is a book about Brazilian music for the drum set made by one of its most advanced modern innovators."
   - Horacio El Negro Hernandez

"Kiko is an artist of the highest caliber. His knowledge, discipline and technique are second to none—but higher than the knowledge and technique is his magnificent and loving soul, intuition, creativity and musical benevolence, all of which are paramount in his artistry every time I hear this beautiful musician play."
   - Gary Husband

At the Portela rehearsal with my brother, the great samba master
Armando Marçal and Charuto.

1986, 15 years old, in search of a dream.

PLAY-ALONG TRACKS

Brasilified

This is a great samba composed by Cliff Korman. The atmosphere is full of energy, dynamics and colors, just like Brasil. Cliff has a beautiful Brazilian heart and I play his tune as an homage to him. Many of the patterns I explain inside this book are here, used in the different parts of the song. The original recording was beautifully played by Brazilian master Paulo Braga and it is an honor to recreate this tune here for you.

Rio

This is a beautiful tune by Nelson Faria, abou the city of Rio de Janeiro—birthplace of bossa nova. The original lyrics talk about the many beautiful landscapes of Rio and about the joy you can feel inside yourself simply by looking at this magical scenery. I try to play inspired by the poetry of the lyrics. Nelson is a partner of many decades, in so many journeys around this world and I feel very happy to play his music here for you. On this track I try to apply many of the subjects worked in this book, always remembering that subtleness is the key to the heart of bossa nova.

Brooklyn High

This is a very special composition by Nelson Faria. It is part of Nosso Trio's CD and DVD *Vento Bravo*. The tune walks through the partido alto and samba styles, with a partido alto groove in the A section and an open samba in the B section. As Nosso Trio is a Brazilian jazz trio, I like to explore new forms and metrics for the comping parts and for my own solo in this piece.

Track 01
♩ = 120

BRASILIFIED
(samba)

Cliff Korman

Brasilified 2/2

Track 04
♩ = 88

RIO
(bossa nova)

Nelson Faria

Rio 2/2

Go to Ⓐ and 2nd ending

Go to Ⓐ Ⓑ Ⓒ Ⓓ for solos.
After solos take 2nd ending and ⊕

BROOKLYN HIGH

Nelson Faria

-1-

-3-

"I had the pleasure of touring together with Kiko Freitas, João Bosco and the NDR Bigband in Brasil in 2007. Since I was just playing the first half of the concert, I got the chance to listen to Kiko´s outstanding grooves every night. His way of playing is very unique, inspiring and tasty all the time. He´s the kind of drummer who always plays what´s right for the song and knows exactly what to do. Kiko has a warm sound on the drums and his touch is simply amazing. Kiko Freitas is one of the most musical drummers I know. I´m his biggest fan!"
    - Wolfgang Haffner

"I have been fortunate to play with Kiko Freitas and those moments rank among the best of my musical life. His ability to listen deeply inside the music and to react instantly to harmonic changes is rare among drummers. He can add color and depth to any musical interaction, while always staying true to the subtleties of the groove. Seeing this book where he lays down in a simple language the foundations of Brazilian grooves has filled me with joy. How many times have we struggled to explain to students the ineffable power of the invisible rhythmic thread that connects musicians who play together as one? This book fills a great void, and it will certainly be appreciated by music students and professionals around the world. Congratulations, Kiko, for this beautiful work of love for the music we all play!"
    - Jovino Santos Neto (Brazilian pianist, composer and educator)

"Having played with Kiko, I can say firsthand that he has a beautiful time feel and is versatile in many styles of music. Kiko is a virtuoso in the truest sense of the word. His technique is always in service of the music! I am excited to study this book because of my deep love for the vast array of grooves from Brazil!"
    - John Patitucci

BONUS VIDEOS

1. IMPRO LIVE B.MP4
• COLORS INSIDE DE SAMBA PULSES OF 4 X 3

This video was recorded during the first sessions of video shooting for this book. Here I try to express the many colors of Afro Brazilian music by using the hands, mallets, brushes and sticks, always searching the deep roots of the culture of my country, throughout the changes of phrasing inside the pulses of 4 and 3.

2. TANAJURA

This is a fantastic composition by João Bosco and Francisco Bosco. My idea here is to create the atmosphere of a little African conversation inside a kitchen, somewhere in the old times of colonial Brasil. Part of the magic here is to try to pulse in 2 over the 7 groove, giving an Afrosamba feel to this great piece. The tune was originally recorded without drum set and it is a challenge to play along with it, without click tracks, trying to recreate the live aspect of the song.

3. IMPRO_1 EM 7/8.MP4
• PAINTING THE 7

This improvise in 7/8 was recorded after we did all the examples of samba groves in odd time signatures. It was just one take and the spirit was to show we can explore the different colors of the drums in a crescent change of shades. To do this I started using one hand and one brush, then two brushes, moving to one brush and one stick, ending with the use of the two sticks, exploring color tones that go from soft dawn to deep and strong day light. Everything was recorded over my own samba brush snare drum pattern.

4. IMPRO_2.MP4
• INNER TIME

The idea here is to let the voice be the inner click and also create lines of phrases over the snare drum brush pattern. Even when I am not singing out loud, I am singing internally the main pulse and also motifs of phrases generating movement to the solo.

5. 4 OVER 3 FREE SOLO
• INNER TIME

This is an open solo where I just try to explore phrases and grooves in a 4 over 3 pulse, even inside the 2/4 snare drum brush pattern. I have fun searching for phrases inside different pulses, instead of just phrasing "inside" the beat- something like exploring chord inversions and outside phrases on a guitar or piano.

KIKO'S SETUP

Setup used for the videos:

PAISTE CYMBALS

- 14" Dark Energy Hi Hats
- 20" Masters Extra Thin
- 8" Alpha Splash (on top of 20" Extra Thin)
- 22" Masters Twenty Dark Ride
- 20" 2002 Wild Crash (with rivets)
- 21" Masters Médium Ride

VIC FIRTH Brushes & Sticks

PEARL - Reference Pure Drums

- 18" bass drum, 12" tom, 14" and 16" floor Toms, Reference snare drum 14/6.5"

ABOUT THE AUTHOR

Kiko Freitas was born in Porto Alegre, Brasil, into a family of musicians, poets and artists, on August 16, 1969. A professional drummer since 1987, he has performed with artists such as Michel Legrand, Nico Assumpção, João Bosco, Milton Nascimento, Chico Buarque, Frank Gambale, Lee Ritenour, John Patitucci, John Beasley, Jeff Richman, Gonzalo Rubalcaba, Jeff Andrews, Hubert Laws, John Leftwich, Wolf Kerschek, Lars Jansson, Nils Landgren, Magnus Lindgren, Peter Asplund, James Genus, Ivan Lins, Hamilton de Holanda, Leila Pinheiro, Armando Marçal, Luiz Eça, Francis Hime, Vladyslav Sendecki, NDR Bigband, Orchestra Jazz Matosinhos, Thomas Törnhaden, Peter Knudsen, Nosso Trio (Nelson Faria & Ney Conceição), OSPA, Orquestra de Câmara do Theatro São Pedro, Renato Borghetti, Baby do Brasil, Frank Solari, Marcelo Corsetti, Alexandre Pires, Itamar Assière, Nico Nicolaiewsky, Guto Wirti, and Ricardo Silveira, among many others.

Photo by Júlio Cordeiro

As an educator, Kiko has presented many clinics in Brazil and around the world, participating as a teacher at schools and events including National Brazilian Drummers Festival, Curso Internacional de Verão-EMB, Masters of the Drums Workshop, Salão Internacional da Bateria, Encontro Latino Americano de Percussão (UFSM), Curitiba Memorial, Conservatório de MPB, Göteborg Music University, Malmö Music University and Stockholm Royal Achademy of Music (Sweden), Hochschule Für Music und Theater- Hamburg, Conservatorium Von Amsterdam, University of Rotherdam, California Jazz Conservatory (USA), Columbus University (Ohio, USA), University of Louisville (Kentucky, USA), Claremont Community School of Music (California, USA).

Kiko has been performing with João Bosco for 20 years, touring extensively in Brazil, the USA and Europe, and performing at many international jazz festivals, such as Schleswig-Holstein-Musik-Festival, Salzau Jazz Festival, Montreaux Jazz Festival, Montreal Jazz Festival, Eldena Jazz Festival, Jazz Baltica, Internacionales Jazz Festival Bingen Swingt, Hamburg Jazz Open, Festival Internacional de Jazz de Granada, Ludwigshafen Enjoy Jazz, Jazz Classics Basel, Jazz Fest Sarajevo, Las Palmas Rincón Jazz, Madrid Jazz Festival, Gijón Festival, All Blues Jazz Recitals, Istanbul Caz Jazz Festival, Kaunas Jazz Festival, Musiques Sur L'ile, Jazz Stars in Krakow, Skopje Jazz Festival, Toulouse Jazz Sur Son, Red Sea Jazz Festival, and Jazz Galicia.

Kiko was voted Best Drummer in World Music by *Modern Drummer* magazine, in 2019. He endorses Vic Firth drumsticks, Paiste cymbals, Pearl drums, Urban Boards drum shoes and Gavazzi cases.

Discography/Reference Music
with Concepts Presented in this Book

João Bosco - *Obrigado Gente* (Kiko Freitas: drums. Samba with tamborim pattern/brushes/odd time samba)
https://open.spotify.com/album/3JRUCJtRyVmcLhUQAxXn7j?si=F9TcH5SvTYiiPVUuv-V5GQ

João Bosco - *40 Anos Depois*
https://open.spotify.com/album/1YiBeU7fqrSFkckEOFEWci?si=7_zSoM7sQ3OB-NwLnXu4Fg

João Bosco - *Na Esquina Ao Vivo*
https://open.spotify.com/album/3PEZgmYBaq6NCTn7nW2Qk5?si=XiNfLDGZTlmAN8y3PbXhzQ

Francis Hime - *Arquitetura da Flor* (Kiko Freitas: drums. Samba with 16th note pulse/bossa nova)
https://open.spotify.com/album/5sSZy7KkA1Aqw4wtVG6Vga?si=XDGGOWYtSZevJ44-O3SR_w

Alon & Joca with NDR Bigband "Arrancada" (Kiko Freitas: Drums. Samba school groove)
https://open.spotify.com/track/4FZVpTmXD6Eq0SCsSIkCPH?si=CpSgTeGLRIOF2CU5MFAxzQ

Alon & Joca with NDR Bigband "Rosas Amarelas" (Kiko Freitas: drums. Samba in 5/4)
https://open.spotify.com/track/3505TOzvcQkUmZHtSmmwWm?si=V-Tw48ZJRbWeu9fIFYECaA

Hermeto Pascoal "Música das Nuvens e do Chão" (Alfredo Dias Gomes: drums. Samba in 7/4)
https://open.spotify.com/track/0ohKztSTnSBUpWOsFN0YHC?si=DiaWWA-fT7CnsJtuHvc_- g

---

"Kiko is a magical musician. His knowledge of rhythm propels the music in a compelling and creative way. He makes everyone in the band sound better. If Kiko lived in the same city as me I would be playing with him all the time."
   - John Beasley

"From the very first time I heard Kiko play, I knew he was a special musician. Besides being an extremely versatile drummer, his impeccable technique is always used in the most musical and tasteful way. He is setting the pace for modern Brazilian drumming with his originality and innovation."
   - Antonio Sanchez

"This latest offering of explaining Brazilian music is so welcome to the drumming community. Why not learn from an expert in this field? Kiko stresses listening and singing what you want to play. This information will take your playing where you want it to be. Thank you for sharing your expertise, Kiko! Now I must return to your ideas—and sing!"
   - Jeff Hamilton